Stories of Li

KNEE
DEEP
AND
RISING

Bob Walkup

outskirtspress
DENVER, COLORADO

Introduction

I've learned the truth that all of us experience the ups and downs of life, some higher and some lower, but definitely the events impact the way we feel or think for years to come. No matter the culture, people tell stories that are both ordinary and extraordinary. Our stories reveal surprising events of human interest and they are filled with both serendipitous joy and crushing defeat.

The characters and events in my life are a colorful kaleidoscope. Sometimes the colors of the characters and events are blended and I can barely distinguish how they have affected my life. But all together they have taught me the nature of peace and violence, tolerance and injustice, love and abuse. They've helped me embrace people who believe in God and also those whose faith takes them down a different path.

A definite result of story writing is that the more I write the more I remember. As my stories have unfolded I've also learned that I, and all of us, are more complicated than we first think. Peeling back the layers of our lives can be a salvation experience. Looking back into my past, near and distant, is like walking into a dimly lit closet and quickly discovering that I'm exploring the subterranean caverns of my deepest and most intriguing thoughts. I've unknowingly crashed into my demons that have had their way with me over the years. I've also met my many lifeguards who have rushed to my side when I needed rescue. On my journey into life I've felt the pain and loss of broken dreams and I've felt the redeeming love of God, restoring my self perception, emancipating my gifts, and empowering me for exceptional accomplishments.

I think that there are only a limited number of stories in the whole world. I believe that my story is everyone's story, the one about birth, love, tragedy, understanding, death and resurrection. I experienced them all by age 12. Every story is all about God, I believe. They are all important. We make a great oversight when we judge our stories as less important than another's. We can't know fully what God is providing for us. That gives us freedom to live out our stories with expectation and hope.

Loretta Bishop has been my inspiration for writing these stories. When I learned that Loretta, my former office administrator and friend at Saint Andrews Presbyterian Church in Raleigh, was diagnosed with a serious cancer I began writing my stories to her in letter form. Her enjoyment of the letters pressed me to consider providing her with more themes that explored the meaning of life. After two years I was looking at 110 finished stories. The 65 stories in "Knee Deep and Rising" are dedicated to Loretta who died February 2, 2011.

Cheryl Spainhour is my friend and editor. I owe the easy flow of the book to her.

May these stories open a few doors into your life. A few names and places have been changed to keep the world a peaceful place.

Bob Walkup

Contents

Growing Up

Maggie

Orangeburg, South Carolina in the 1950's had plenty of problems like segregation that I as a ten-year old boy didn't know anything about other than the fact that my Dad and Mom would drive my family through colored town on Sunday afternoons so we could make fun at the black people coming out of church all dressed up. The men wore black suits and the women were dressed in white dresses like they were ready for the Lord to come again. I secretly thought it just might happen one day and they would be the first to be called up yonder. They were so happy coming down the church steps at Tabernacle Baptist, not like the folks at my Presbyterian church where everybody seemed somber about the whole religious thing. I never could figure out the black folks, how they could get such a thrill out of church.

I was taught early on that God made white people and they were supposed to be in charge of the black people and that's all there was to it. When we would ride by their church they would wave and bow a little in moderate humility. I remember sometimes feeling more important than they were. Black children my age didn't bow to us though. They seemed to know something we didn't. They had looks of determination and courage on their faces. I didn't know what the future would hold for me or for them, but I felt uncomfortable about it all.

In Kissam's Grocery the blacks had to wait their turns until the white people had shopped and checked out first. In Belk's the blacks shopped in the basement, not primarily because there were cheaper goods there but because they could be separated from the whites. There were two different water fountains, one for whites and one for blacks. Black people always had to step aside if a white person came down the aisle.

To tell the truth, it never came to mind during all of the days when I played sports at Adden Street Park that there were no black kids on our teams. Neither did it cross my mind to find out where they played together. As far as I knew the city didn't spend any money for a park for the black folks at all. Maybe the spirit of the black folks didn't let the lack of a playground keep them from having fun anyway. But the discrimination in schools in my town must have been terribly oppressive because as a twelve-year old I never saw a black school, not because they weren't there to see, but because my parents probably didn't want me to see how run down they were.

There was one black woman who seemed like a member of our family. She came to clean our house and wash our clothes and I loved her more than any other woman than Mom. My Mom said it just wasn't right for black people to come in a white person's front door since it might look like they're being accepted by us on equal terms. It was hard for me to understand why Maggie wasn't allowed to eat at our kitchen table with us. She had to wait until we had completed our meal before sitting down for her meal. When the weather was mild she would eat on the back porch but not until we had finished ours in the kitchen. Maggie Johnson was short and chubby with an almost toothless smile that warmed my heart every time she knocked on our back door.

Dad said that black people had to stay in their place and not get uppity. I don't know why Dad called the black people Negroes sometimes but then when he was angry he called them niggers or darkies. I don't know what it was back then but even as a young boy I could feel a sadness in my soul when my Dad talked that way. It seemed ironic that when Dad would occasionally take Maggie home after she had worked all day at our house, he wouldn't let her sit in the front seat because it might appear that she was equal to him or that he had a friend who was a nigger. Yet when Maggie was asked to sit in the back seat it actually appeared that Dad was the chauffer of a rich lady, which in hindsight catches me as hilarious.

Even with a house full of prejudice I knew in my boyhood years that there was something that set Maggie apart from other black people and from other white people as well. She helped my Mom raise my brothers and me. On many occasions she would baby sit for us while our parents went to a Friday night movie at the Carolina Theater. She even sat in my Dad's big, comfy chair while they were gone, whether Dad knew it or not. I never knew whether she could read or not but she looked at the newspapers and asked us questions about what the white people were doing in town. There was no news about the black people in the Times and Democrat paper, even though there were two black schools there, South Carolina State and Claflin College.

Prejudice in Orangeburg boiled over in 1968 when students from State and Claflin staged a march from their schools to a "white only" bowling alley where they wanted the right to play. They tried to leave the campus and were warned to turn back. But they were determined to have what the Constitution guaranteed to all Americans. Law enforcement officers from the state began firing on them, killing three and wounding 27 students. It was the darkest day in Orangeburg's history. I was in my first year at Lakewood Presbyterian Church in Jacksonville, Florida when the massacre occurred. I never heard a word about the violence. I wonder if one of Maggie's children was one of those who died.

In my college years the memory of Maggie in the comfy chair triggered a remarkable sight and smell of my past. I remembered that Mom told me that Maggie breast-fed me sometimes when Mom couldn't provide me with breast milk. Maggie held me close and breast-fed me!

Amazing! Is that why I have a natural affection for blacks today?

It's reasonable that today I love black people as much as I do white people. It's unreasonable to think I could feel any other way. However, when recently reading a letter I wrote in my sophomore year of college, I crashed into the painful truth that my prejudice in the 60's was self-evident, regardless of how hard I fought my internal battle to be free. More than I like to admit, my cultural heritage bound me to a value system that excluded blacks from equality. My prejudice lasted until the day I heard Martin Luther King, Jr. speak in Atlanta during my seminary years. Is it reasonable to think that the world will one day be able to see the glorious peace that comes from knowing that God breast-feeds all of us every day?

Wheezing For Breath

Our childhood living room was in a small home with asbestos siding. The room included a piano that my Mother played by ear after supper each night. There was a straight chair by the piano. No one ever wanted to sit on it. It was too hard to enjoy. There were two large, comfortable chairs too. One was by the front door, and the other one stood across from the piano. It was my Dad's chair. I think the reason Dad picked that chair to sit in was so that he could watch Mom play the piano without her knowing that he was idolizing her. It was next to the large upright Philco radio with a record player beneath it. Dad's chair left room between it and the radio, room for my two brothers and me to squeeze into while listening to the scores of the Yankees and the Dodgers games.

If "The Shadow Knows" were on the air we would squeeze together like sardines in a can on our backs with our faces looking up to a magazine or a newspaper. Dad's hand moved above our faces with his lighted cigarette on the way to the big, round ashtray on top of the radio. It seemed Dad always had a Kool cigarette in his hand, He never held one between his lips like some of the fellows at church did. Clouds of smoke drifted down on us from his cigarettes. Smoke was like the organdy curtains in our living room: it just hung around. It seemed to lie down upon us. It was always there. But it was our home and our culture and I never gave it much thought. I don't think any of us did.

While lying on the floor with my brothers, John and Bill, I often coughed a lot. Then I would begin to wheeze. I had a hard time breathing as a boy. So I would have to leave the radio party and go into the kitchen so that my coughing and wheezing wouldn't interfere with my brothers' enjoyment. The hardest part of the day and night was going to bed because when I lay down my wheezing got worse. Mom would have me sit up in the bed, which seemed to help a bit sometimes. Getting my breath was like breathing through a dishtowel. I had to work to breathe.

Our family doctor, Doctor Whitzman, was a regular visitor to our home during the critical times. He was a big man, short but fat, and when my Mom would usher him into my bedroom the floor would creak and so would my bed when he sat on it. He would check my chest with his stethoscope and flash his mysterious light into my eyes. I always wondered what he knew about me that nobody else did. Then he'd give me some ipecac, a drug designed to help my respiration. I suppose it did since I'm here reporting about it. But Doctor Whitzman had an interesting smell about him. It wasn't shaving lotion or fried chicken, which I'm sure he ate his portion of. The smell was like my Dad. Whitzman was a smoker too. He breathed like he had been running through our neighborhood. I think maybe he needed some ipecac too.

I look back on Dad and Doctor Whitzman, two of the most important men in my life, without any anger. Neither of them knew anything about the relationship between smoking and respiratory illnesses. I have wished for a healthier childhood. I spent too many nights ailing, to some extent the immediate result of smoke inhalation, but I fully believe that if Dad could have known how his smoking affected my health he never would have smoked in our home. His dedicated years on the job to provide us all that we needed, including medical care and medicines, reminds me that he loved us all. We might have lived in a smoky home but it was a good one. We had everything we needed, but clean air.

And besides, when I look back on my wheezing I did get an extra dose of love from Mom during those long nights of troubled sleep. Everybody would be asleep but her and me. I suppose that my respiratory weakness served as a passageway through which she and I loved each other and bonded together more than I can imagine. That bond split from time to time, usually due to her emotional stress.

Mom experienced deep depressions and frightening anxiety. I was her caregiver during my college years, which were some of her worse days. Frankly, in hindsight those were some very hard days for me too. I look back and I can see that I was borderline bipolar. My own emotional state was growing toward the kind that Mom was feeling. I gave her all that I had which was not enough. She gave life her best during those days but she didn't have effective medicines or an adequate support group until she was an older adult. She died 15 years ago. I think we could have a wonderful time sitting and talking together today.

Santa Claus

Anne and I are gearing up for our second Christmas with Nathan and Lydia, our grandchildren, who haven't quite figured out this whole Santa Claus thing yet. It's challenging to teach them about Advent, Christmas and Santa Claus. It's rather confusing actually.

One of my fondest memories of Christmas happened when I was age 5. My Dad told me and my 7 year old brother, Bill, that if we peeked and saw Santa come to the door (we didn't have a fireplace) that Santa wouldn't leave any toys for us. We were told to stay in our beds if we heard Santa coming to our house. So when a truck loudly stopped in front of our home, its muffler popping like gunshots, Bill and I stayed in our beds until the mystery pushed us over the edge. We slowly crept out of our beds and peeked through the curtains to get our first glimpse of the bearded wonder in a red suit. There he was. What a surprise! Coming to our door from a truck that had "Johnson's Hardware Store" written on the door was a man dressed in overalls and he was black. Bill and I couldn't believe our eyes. Santa Claus visited our door for at least several more years but we never let on that we knew he was black and from a local store. When I told my friends about Santa Claus nobody believed me. And our parents may have known that we knew the real truth about Santa too but nobody owned up to it. The reality game would have been no fun at all and serve no purpose. Meanwhile the true Christmas meaning took on more power year after year. There is a time and place for both fantasy and reality for both children and adults.

The Water Tower

When I was a boy I did things every boy did, like riding my bike, skating down the driveway, and playing monopoly with my brothers when it rained. But I also looked for things I had been warned not to do, dangerous things that I thought I could do without anyone knowing about them. Of course, doing them with a friend made our stunts even more fun.

I was ten and my neighbor, Stewart Hill, was nine when it all happened. We got tired of playing baseball with the older kids in the big vacant lot down the street, so we decided to play catch together under the water tower that was across the street from Stewart's house. We walked under the tower, which stood like a giant balloon over us. Tall thatch grew as high as our shoulders and almost concealed us from Stewart's sisters playing in their front yard. We stomped down a path between us to help us see one another clearly and began to throw the baseball back and forth.

While baseball was my favorite sport, boredom set in and my mind shifted to the ladder that was about 8 feet above the ground and extended to the top of the tower some 150 feet high. After a brief discussion with Stewart that was filled with both devilment and ignorance we decided that I would be the one who could reach the ladder and climb to the top of the tower. Since Stewart had a partial paralysis on his left side from polio, he didn't have the physical strength to climb the tower.

Stewart leaned over and grabbed his knees. I climbed on his back and stood as high as I could but I couldn't reach the water tower steps. Stewart ran to his house and brought back their stepladder. I climbed the ladder and stretched myself high enough to reach the bottom rung of the water tower's ladder. I pulled up like I was on vertical monkey bars until I could get my feet on the first rung. I made it. I felt like I was a grown-up, doing things men do. Stewart urged me to climb as high as I could and tell him what I could see. I scurried up the tower, rung by rung, without stopping to look down. It was exciting to see my friends playing ball down the block and to see over Stewart's house to mine. I was as tall as the roofs of the houses in the neighborhood. I looked down to where Stewart was standing and was shocked to see how high I had climbed. It was a very long way to the bottom. My hands trembled. I wondered if I could hold on. I needed to carefully climb down the 20 steps I'd taken as quickly as possible. From the bottom rung I jumped into the tall thatch. Never would I climb the tower again.

We sat down and talked a few minutes about how somebody needed to sew our baseball back together since the cover was beginning to unravel and come apart. I don't think we would have talked about girls because they were too silly and sweet smelling to spend any time with. I have to admit that I played with Stewart's little sister, Tamara, once or twice when my brothers weren't around. I never told anyone about it or they would have teased me to death. That's when it hit me. We needed to have some fun that both of us could enjoy. I pulled a short string of firecrackers out of my pocket, saved from July 4th. The fun was about to begin.

I didn't have any matches. Stewart said he knew where his Dad kept them for his pipe smoking. Off he ran to his house and flew back as fast as his handicap would let him go. Stewart lit a match and tossed it into the tall grass. When the grass flame flared up I lighted a firecracker and threw it into the middle of the burning grass. It blew out the fire in the grass. It worked several times. We laughed over our new discovery and felt very proud of ourselves. On the next throw my firecracker failed to blow out the fire in the grass. Instead it sent fire in several different directions. Stewart and I began stomping the shoulder high flames that now were leaping in the grass all around us.

It quickly became clear to us that the flames were too hot for us to extinguish. We agreed that our situation was an emergency that required sharp thinking. We ran for our lives, leaving the ladder behind! Stewart went into his garage and I ran past him to mine. For some reason I decided that my safest place would be under my bed. So I sneaked in the back door, through the kitchen, and slid under my bed as quietly as I could. I made it. Nobody saw me. No one would ever know where I was. But the football, skates, shoes and BB gun made it hard for me to get comfortable.

The siren in the distance, coming closer every minute, made my hot, sweaty back shiver like someone had put a piece of ice down my shirt. Surely the fire had gone out on its own and the truck was heading to another neighborhood, not mine. The siren got closer and closer. Then the fire truck roared past our home, screeched around the corner back to Dantzler Avenue where the fire in the field under the tower was burning. From the sound of many feet running past our home I could tell that most everybody in the neighborhood on that Saturday afternoon was going to the fire, wondering how it got started.

After what seemed like a whole week the backdoor opened and shut with the sound of conviction. It was the sound my Dad made when he intended to get things done. I could see his shoes heading through the kitchen. His heavy footsteps led to the foot of my bed, halting suddenly like a drill sergeant on parade. I held my breath for an eternity, unaware that the smoke on my clothes was a dead giveaway to my location. Then it happened, Dad asked with a loud voice if

I had started the fire? I gasped for breath and confessed my sin but not because I thought that telling the truth would cut me any slack in discipline. It was just that Dad had taught me to tell the truth, no matter what. Firmly he called me out from under my bed. I hung my head in shame before him. When he lifted my chin up and our eyes met I could see his great disappointment in me. He commended me for telling the truth and I hoped it might lessen the punishment that I was certain was coming my way.

Dad took off his belt. It was a big belt. He asked me how many trucks answered the fire at the water tower. I told him I heard only one. Dad agreed that there was one and asked me to drop my pants and lean over the bed. I'm going to give you only one belting but it will be one that you'll remember all of your life. To this day I remember that one lick on my butt. From that day forward I never played with fire, or cursed too often, or did a million things a boy can think of to do, except skip church a few times.

Fun Games With Black Kids

When my family climbed into our 1948 green Plymouth and headed to my favorite Uncle Norwood's farm near Bishopville, S.C. everyone anticipated a wonderful time. My Mom and Dad looked forward to sitting on the front porch with my Uncle Norwood and Aunt Nan. The wrap-around porch was shaded in the front by a grand old oak tree that looked as if it might have been planted by Columbus in 1492. Mom and Dad would sit with Norwood and Nan for hours talking about whatever grownups talk about, like the President's slow development of the economy, the Yankees and the Dodgers race toward the World Series, and of course, children and what to do with them so they'll grow up and get a job, if there is one to have. It must have been boring to just sit there and talk all day.

As for me and my brothers, Bill and John, we had a great time playing together with Uncle Norwood's children, Esther and Mary, who were about my age, perhaps eight and ten years old. I know they went to school in town but they lived in the country so that made them country girls. On the other hand it was what they did when they got home that made them country girls. They played with the black kids who lived with their parents in houses on Uncle Norwood's farm. The Negro parents worked the farm planting corn and picking cotton. The black kids worked the farm too, as much as they were able.

But when Esther and Mary wanted playmates they didn't have far to go. So when my brothers and I arrived at the farm, the first thing Esther and Mary did was to shout for their farm friends to come and play. Out of the door they would run. I can't remember how many kids there were but I think there were seven. Some of their names and nicknames were Mike, Pooter, Squirrel, Annie May and Fox. Their

Dad was Ransom. He was in charge of the farm. Their Mom, Pearl, did the housework and cooked for Esther and Mary's family.

It didn't take long to decide on the games we would play. I loved baseball so we played baseball first, only we didn't have a ball or a bat. The black kids taught us how to make a ball by pouring sand into a sock and tying off the leg of the sock. For a bat we used a fat stick. It was some of the most enjoyable baseball (sock ball) I had ever played. Watching the black kids and Esther and Mary play made me wish they were on my Little League team back in Orangeburg.

For more exercise we had foot races from Esther and Mary's home down to the black kids' home. I learned that they were faster than I was. John and Bill could barely keep up with them but in their bare feet they were quick as lightning. Perhaps more fun than a foot race was racing with the old car tires. The black kids pushed discarded tires around the yard and down the path to their home and back. They also were capable of turning the tires in a circle by pushing on the side of the tire treads. It took me a while to learn how to work the tires but when I did it seemed more enjoyable than riding a bike, or perhaps it was the novelty of it. But I think that I enjoyed most our play time in the barn which was a cavernous building filled with equipment like a tractor and plows, tools of every kind, many which baffled me since I'd never seen anything like them before. And we always laughed the most in the barn while playing in the high piled cottonseed in the huge bin. We jumped in the soft seed like it was a giant pillow. We stuffed cottonseed in each other's pants and laughed until we were out of breath.

When it was dinnertime, the black kids asked us to help them catch a chicken to eat. The chicken chosen was fast enough that we couldn't catch him. So we all began throwing rocks to kill him. It seems mean

15

today but in that day it was the same as going to the grocery store. They needed the meat and raised the chickens as part of their regular diet. When we finally slowed the chicken down enough to catch him, their Dad, Ransom, chopped his head off with a hatchet and their Mom fried him. They all licked their lips. I did too. It smelled good. When it was time for them to eat they all gathered around a small table and divided up the meat so that everybody had a share. But I've got to say that what happened next I had never seen and will unlikely see again. As the boys and girls finished each piece of chicken they threw their chicken bones behind the stove. I don't know if they were doing that to entertain us, but it did make us laugh out loud. If Pearl had seen their antics I'm sure she would have gotten after them with a switch.

When our Mom and Dad called us to go home we were sad because we were having such a great time. We learned that we didn't need a bat and ball, just a sock full of sand and a stick to play baseball with. We didn't need a bicycle. All we needed were a couple of old tires to roll. And an old barn was as good as a playground back home. Cottonseed offered a hundred laughs. Maybe the toys and activities back in town didn't have the value they once did for us. We'll always remember our two country cousins and their black friends. Life couldn't be better than when we visited them.

Hurry, Get My Wig

When I was in the 4th grade at Ellis Avenue Grammar School in Orangeburg,S.C. one of my best friends was Jay Rousseau who sat in the desk in front of me in a row of desks that must have been 7 or 8 deep. Our desks were the closest ones to the tall windows on our left. It was a good class. I can still remember being a good reader and winning almost every spelling bee. And if I didn't win, then Jay would. It was important to beat Jay in the contest because whoever lost in the spelling bee had to give a marble to the winner, and neither of us liked giving up our prized possessions that were almost always the center of attention at recess.

But I also remember being slow on the draw in our math tests. The whole class would stand near the blackboard up front and the teacher, Mrs. Ellison, a pretty lady who always dressed like she was going to church, would give us the problems to answer. She always played with her hair a lot, like putting pins and things in it and I guess I never really knew why. But I do know that I liked the problems to answer like 8x7 and 9x 8 but I hoped she wouldn't get around to asking me for the answers for problems like 7x76 and 9x88. I usually had to sit down when there were 5 or 6 kids still standing. Early on I knew that I wasn't heading towards science or engineering. My friend, Jay had about the same math aptitude as I did and usually sat down about the same time as I did. That took a little of the embarrassment out of defeat.

One day as Mrs. Ellison walked back and forth near the windows from the front to the back of the classroom, calling out math problems to the last two contestants in a math bee, she opened one of the windows of our second floor classroom. A quick rush of spring wind came in and out of our room and Mrs. Ellison's wig flew out with it. I didn't even know there was something called a wig but I learned right away that there was. "Robert and Jay, run quickly and bring me back my hair," she pleaded. Well, we could see how troubled she was with her head hanging out the window covered up by her hands. We ran as fast as we could down two flights of stairs and began searching for her wig among the hedges that lined the brick wall in front of the school. It was nowhere to be found. We looked on top of the hedges and on the ground around them. No wig! About that time Mrs. Ellison in desperation said, "If you find it quickly you don't have to do any math homework for 2 days."

Why didn't she say that in the first place? We put 2 and 2 together and suddenly our hunt took on emergency status. We found her wig caught deep in the hedge and quickly retrieved it like a Labrador brings home a duck. We flew up the stairs like Superman. When we handed the wig to our teacher she said to the class, "Nobody look, it's not funny." As she tried to replace the wig I still remember her real hair being okay like it was. I couldn't tell why she wore the wig at all. Everybody in the class talked about that day for years but for Jay and me, being exempt from math homework for two nights was better than a chocolate cake, and I love cake.

Leroy Pew, That's For Sure

Leroy usually came to school without any shoes. All of my first grade friends and I thought how lucky he was that he could come skipping into class with his bare feet like he was a clown in the circus. Since the circus never came to a little town like Orangeburg, I suppose Leroy was the best we could get. I sometimes asked our teacher, Miss Stephenson, if we could take off our shoes too. But usually before I could complete my sentence she would shush me down to keep all my friends from begging too. Not only did Leroy skip like a clown but he also dressed like one. His pants came down past his knees but not more than an inch or two. They hardly gathered around his waist where the button at the top couldn't reach its buttonhole. Leroy always had some cool shirts too. I wished I could have had some faded shirts like Leroy's. Somehow I never quite understood why clothes meant so much to people anyway. I liked his haircut because it was cut the same, short length all over his head.

He sat next to me at the table in the back of the class. That was good because Miss Stephenson knew that he needed some extra help. I was a good reader so I got to help him along. Leroy didn't know the difference between "sky" and "ball." He confused "go" and "stop" and couldn't keep up with the class. But I helped him along with his assignments as best I could. I was always curious why somebody couldn't read, even a little. I asked him if his Dad read books to him at home. He said his Dad left home long ago. He said his Mom didn't read to him because she had so many children to care for. He told me they lived on Cemetery Lane, the road across the street from the Presbyterian Church. Since I was a Presbyterian I knew exactly where Cemetery Lane was but I didn't think we had any poor kids from that street coming to our church. I didn't know why since our church was so close by.

I think the only thing I didn't like about Leroy was his stinky odor, day after day. I nicknamed him Leroy Pew but I never called him that to anybody else since it might hurt his feelings. Most of my class didn't want to get close to him. Before I came to first grade I had never been around anyone like Leroy. I could smell him from four or five feet away. When I asked him if he ever took a bath he said that every Wednesday was his day and he hated to get in the big old tub because the water was so cold. On Wednesday he was the second to get in, right behind his big brother who must have used up all the hot water. I knew something about taking baths after my two older brothers too. But when the water in our tub got cold we would just turn the hot water knob and out came a warm up. I had the feeling that Leroy's house might not have hot water at all.

Stink and all, I loved playing with Leroy during recess. I was the fastest runner in the first grade, except for Leroy. At least twice during every recess Leroy would challenge me to race from the school steps to the picnic table at the far end of the schoolyard. He would let me run right beside him until the very last minute and then he would burst ahead to win. The picnic table was under a shed with a tin roof. The table was about eight feet by eight feet and made of wood. It was about two feet high. As far as the boys were concerned the table was not for picnicking, it was where we played "King On The Mountain." Now playing this game meant that we would all climb onto the table and begin pushing our classmates off to the dirt below. The last boy standing was the King On The Mountain. I don't remember how many kids broke an arm or fingers in the recess free-for-all but we played it throughout the year. I was agile and won many times but it was Leroy who was the strongest and the King more than I. Maybe his winning ways also had something to do with the fact that nobody wanted to touch Leroy Pew.

Every Christmas the King's Daughters Organization, a service club for ladies, would hand out to its members the name of a poor family to help out. So I went with Mom to the grocery store to buy rice, potatoes, beans and probably some apples and oranges too. She made a chocolate cake for sure. That was her favorite and mine too. Then we went to Belk's Store and bought shirts and sweaters for seven children and a coat for the mom in the house where the poor people lived. We wrapped the presents and loaded the food and clothing into our car and headed out to distribute the Christmas things. When we turned past the side of the cemetery down Cemetery Lane I knew that Leroy lived on that street but I didn't know which house. It didn't occur to me that we might be paying a Christmas visit to his family.

So when Mom stopped the car we carried everything to the porch before knocking on the door. When Leroy opened the door he saw me and grinned just enough to show that he recognized me. Leroy stepped back to make room for his Mom, Mrs. Sylette, as she came to the door. My Mom explained who we were and why we were there and Mrs. Sylette reluctantly invited us to come in. With the children's help we brought the Christmas gifts inside. There we were in the smallest house I'd ever been in and my friend, Leroy lived there. There were gaps between the wooden walls, letting in the winter's wind. The pot bellied stove had wood burning in it but it had to fight to keep the house warm. As I counted the seven children, Leroy came closer to me and asked what I wanted for Christmas. I said I didn't know because I didn't want to make him feel bad.

When the family finished opening their gifts my Mom shared with them a devotional message about Jesus. Mrs. Sylette thanked us many times during our 15 minute visit. When we opened the door to leave, I looked at Leroy and smiled. He didn't smile back. Maybe he was shocked to get such a nice gift. He might have felt too embarrassed to smile since I had seen how poor his family was. As we walked down his front steps to our car Leroy told me that he'd see me at school again soon.

I went through the Christmas Holidays with a different set of eyes. I realized for the first time that my family was rich. We had plenty of heat and food and hot water. We were rich. That event at Leroy's home probably softened my heart more than any other one event for years to come. It may be the source of my life of service to not only the rich but also to the poor.

Uncle Luke

My silver-haired Uncle Luke rolled his 1950 Ford onto our Orange-burg dirt driveway about every six weeks. I usually jumped off the front porch and ran fast enough to greet him beside his car before he had time enough to cut his engine off. Uncle Luke and I went through the same loving ritual every time. He'd open his car door, reach down and lift me up until we were face to face. "I love you, Robert," he would boom with the deepest voice in the whole world. I felt like heaven had come to visit me. I scissored his belly with my dirty Little League uniform and he hugged me like a big Teddy Bear, once on the left cheek and once on the right. His late afternoon stubble didn't bother me. I can still smell the Old Spice Lotion that he splashed on his face early morning back in Charlotte. He smelled like he was ready for something, I didn't know what. I do know that he was the nearest thing to perfect.

When my brothers arrived beside Uncle Luke's Ford they got the same royal treatment I did, bear hugs and all. He loved us all the same, well maybe he loved me just a little bit more. My brothers and I tussled to be the one who would carry his suitcase from the car into the house. Being the little guy, I always lost the suitcase game, but it really didn't matter since I got to hold hands with him as we walked up the front steps. Mom and Dad welcomed him with open arms and ushered him through the screen door. After supper he would tell us tales about all the interesting places he had been and the curious people he had met. Uncle Luke was a traveling salesman who seemed to love most everybody. After supper he would gather us around the coffee table in the living room for gift time. He'd give Dad a shirt, Mom an apron, and sports equipment to us kids. Then came the gift we waited for, a box of Hershey Bars.

When it was bedtime my brother Bill and I moved out of our bedroom so that Uncle Luke could sleep there. It was good to make room for him. Perhaps that's what Jesus meant in John 14:23, "If you love me, the Father and I will come and make a home in you."

Stained Glass

My faith in God is so multi-faceted that it is impossible for me to pull together all of the people and happenings that make my faith vital today. One of them stands out today, perhaps because I was reminiscing about my childhood last night with my brothers at my birthday party. It happened most every Sunday in our small Presbyterian Church in Orangeburg, S.C. When I was age 4 thru approximately 10 years old I would have to sit between my Dad and Mom in worship to keep me and my brothers from giggling about most anything. I liked going to worship. I liked to hear the organ and choir. As far as I was concerned, the choir members were angels who came to visit us from heaven each Sunday morning. When the ushers came down the aisle like soldiers marching to war I sat up real straight so they wouldn't pick me out of the crowd and take me with them. The preacher's voice was as low as "Swing Low, Sweet Chariot," and the rhythm of his speech was comforting, almost to the point of putting me to sleep. Occasionally I did, but there was something about the whole service that instilled in me a heart for God from an early age.

The only thing about church that I didn't like was the hats. I promise you, every woman wore a hat the size of Big Ben's clock. If I wanted to see anything in church I had to get my fill of it as I came down the aisle to take my seat in the pew between my parents. I couldn't see anything but a big purple hat and a fire engine red hat on the ladies in front of me. So I usually gave up around the sermon time and lay down in my Mom's lap. But something interesting then happened. From my Mom's lap I had a perfect angle to see under the purple and red hats and over the heads of the choir to a perfect view of the stained glass window. There he was, Jesus with his arms spread wide enough to shepherd in all the children and adults around the world.

His face was warm and loving and the adults and children seemed so joyful and comfortable in his presence. I couldn't see the minister but I could hear his words. I could understand enough of them to believe that my stained glass Jesus would say something much like the preacher was saying.

I haven't visited my childhood church since I left Orangeburg in 1953 at age 12. Probably the sanctuary and the choir loft have been expanded to accommodate more people in worship. Probably the aisle has been given a new foundation to keep it from squeaking so much when the ushers walk down to receive the offering. But I believe that even with all the changes that have taken place over the last 56 years that the stained glass window is just the same. I hope to visit again soon on a Sunday and when I do I'm going to sit behind a few hat ladies again. Then I'm going to lie down in the pew to see if Jesus still talks and looks the way he use to when I was a boy.

Hide and Seek

Hide and Seek has got to be the most universal game in the world. I played it with children in Congo and South Korea. I had some hilarious games with children in Bangkok and rural Bangladesh that broke down the cultural and language differences that attempted to wall us apart. But playing Hide and Seek combines the elements of mystery and surprise, making the game the most popular one for children everywhere.

When I was a child in Orangeburg, S.C. I played Hide and Seek with my brothers and our neighborhood friends. It was our favorite game in the early evening when the moon was beginning to rise. The neighborhood boys, maybe a dozen or so, liked to gather in front of our home. There were only boys, you see, not one girl lived on our block. When one of the older boys volunteered to be the "Seeker" the rest of us scattered like doves at the blast of a shotgun. Our hiding places were behind shrubs, high on tree limbs and under houses. Some of us hid behind a car or in a dark corner near the back porch.

But not me, my favorite hiding place was in the backyard storage room, which was off limits. The storage room was adjacent to our garage, which was too unsafe to park our car in. We never knew when it would sag a bit more and collapse into a heap. Inside the 8 feet by 8 feet storage room the ceiling was no higher than seven feet. A rake, a shovel and a pick stood on their wooden handles in the back corner. On the left side of the storage room there was a little used axe and a hoe that Mama used to dig in the soil to soften it for planting tomato seeds near the back porch. On the right side, old rusty, bike wheels and buckets with broken handles lay flat on the floor. There was an old table that had a small bag of fertilizer and a giant can full of nails on it, plus most anything somebody had in their hands and needed a place for. A croaker sack full of wood leaned against the wall, which seemed strange since we only had a kerosene heater in the hallway of our house. A box of old newspapers was near the door so that it wouldn't open but halfway. There were no windows and the light cord was popped off at the socket. It was pretty dark in there, even in the middle of the day.

One night when the guys began the game we scattered quickly to our hiding places. I took the long way around my house to throw off Jimmy, the Seeker. Since no one had ever found me in the storage room I felt safe to hide there again. I quickly pried opened the door that squeaked like an old door will do, squeezed inside and then I squeaked it closed most of the way, leaving a 12" crack so that I could see out into the moonlit driveway. I slipped in past the wood and the newspapers and could feel the rake and shovel in the corner. It was always a dark hiding place but on that night the moon ducked behind the clouds and I could barely see through the cracked door into the yard outside. Jimmy came by a couple of times looking for the guys but didn't dare come into my dark den. I knew that I had the best hiding place in the neighborhood.

I stood there thinking about how cool it was that no one but I would enter the dark room. And I also laughed under my breath at all the obvious places some of the other kids would choose to hide, only to be quickly found. Yet I had an unusual feeling that night. There was a slight rustle in the back of the storage room. I knew that it was a mouse in the newspapers. Funny when you get a little spooky how your mind can wander a little. My heart beat a little faster but I figured that it was just from the adrenaline rush of the Hide and Seek game.

Outside, the moon slid from behind the clouds making it just light enough for Jimmy to seek out another player and say "gotcha", to one of the kids he had found. Inside the storage room I began to feel restless, believing that Jimmy and the rest of the guys had gotten tired of looking for me and had stopped playing the game. Meanwhile I felt a small breeze on the back of my neck and wondered how a breeze could move on such a still, summer night.

I adjusted my feet and tripped on the bag of wood, which knocked over the hoe and the axe. Feeling a little edgy I stood back up again and collected myself. That's when I felt a little breeze again, only this time it was hotter than before. I slowly turned around and, "Gotcha" whispered the voice in the dark. I screamed and ran for my life. Some monster had almost caught me and I had escaped by the skin of my teeth.

At that moment I probably could have outrun all the boys on the block, regardless of their ages. When I got back to the front yard where the rest of the boys had gathered they were all laughing at me. That's when my brother Bill came around the corner laughing over the way he scared me in the storage room. The boys had set me up on a trick that took me at least an hour to get over.

Hide and Seek is the best game in the world.

It's Amazing I Made It Through Christmas

Our tree this year is a grandchildren's tree, loaded with non-breakable ornaments so that Nathan and Lydia can pull off the ones they want. Seeing Christmas through kids' eyes is a fresh new experience for us. It gives us freedom to let our minds wander wherever they choose to go.

Today my mind wanders to the wonders of my boyhood during Christmas. I really don't know how I ever made it from one Christmas to the next because of all the things you'd get. For instance, I once read in a comic book ad that I could order stuff like bar bells and become a "He Man" with huge muscles or maybe get a magician's wand and turn my dog into a duck. But the item that made my fingers tingle was a "real replica of a Civil War cannon, 15 inches long." But wait, there's more. The iron cannon had an opening in the back of the barrel where you could put real gunpowder. After closing the barrel, there was a switch that sparked the powder which produced enough "boom" to be heard by all of your friends," the ad said. So there I was, ten years old, ordering the most dangerous thing in the comic book. That's right, I had knocked down enough mistletoe out of the trees to sell in my neighborhood and I had made enough money to cover the $2.95 for the cannon.

The three weeks before the cannon arrived were not wasted though. In my neighborhood on Carolina Avenue there were 15 boys and 3 girls within a one-block area. So if there was something that anybody could think of to do, we did it together. We often gathered in front of somebody's house during the Christmas season to explode firecrackers. That was fun but I think it was more fun when the crowd cleared out and just I and my 12 year old brother, Bill, and my 16 year old brother, John, would be left to shoot firecrackers by ourselves. We didn't put the firecrackers in the grass and light them with a match. That was too easy. We would drip tallow from a candle onto the front steps and place the candle upright in the hot tallow so it would stand on its own. Then out of our pockets we would bring a few dozen firecrackers. It was risky but fun to hold a firecracker in my hand, then place the firecracker stem in the candle flame to light it. Immediately the powder would ignite. Our game was seeing how long you could hold the firecracker before you threw it! Almost always my timing on the burning fuse was right, but when I misjudged it the firecracker would go off near my fingers. I would holler and cry, but never enough to cause our Dad to come out and make us find something else to do. It's amazing I made it through Christmas.

If that wasn't enough, my next-door neighbor, Pat DesChamps, liked to play with powder too. But he was a serious bomb maker. We would all gather around him on his front porch and watch him take the powder from maybe 40 firecrackers and pour it into a soup can, stuff newspaper on top of it, and design a long stem to light the bomb with. Then he would check to make sure that none of our parents were looking. When the coast was clear Pat would place the bomb on the sidewalk, light it, and we would all run for cover behind a post or around the corner of Pat's house. I usually took cover behind the big pecan tree in my yard next door. The "barrooooom" of it always surprised and thrilled us. But on one occasion when the bomb exploded, Pat was peeking his head around a front porch pole to see the bomb go off and the explosion sent a piece of the soup can sailing at Pat, cutting his throat badly enough that he had to go to the hospital to get stitched up. It was amazing any of us made it through Christmas.

At last my cannon arrived. It was on my birthday, December 22nd. My Dad let me take it out of the box and wow, it was everything I had hoped it would be. It was made of metal and must have weighed a sturdy 4 or 5 pounds. I placed the cannon on the ground. Dad watched over me as I unwrapped the box of powder and put the powder in the proper depository at the rear of the cannon barrel. He showed me how to close the barrel and explained how to make a spark. There I was with the ultimate "bang machine." With excitement I turned the spark switch for the first time and "Pow", the cannon broke the silence of the neighborhood almost as loud as Pat's homemade bombs. All of my friends came running from their homes, as excited as they might have been if Jesus was lying in a manger in my front yard. For at least 3 days I was the most popular kid on the block, until the powder ran out. I tried to make the firecracker powder work in the cannon but it just fizzled out. When we called the cannon company to order more powder they said it was sold out and wouldn't be offered anymore due to the fact that so many kids were being hurt when the cannon cracked. It's amazing I ever made it through Christmas!

Footnote: My friend, Pat, the bomb maker, eventually attended The Citadel and graduated as a specialist in armaments and demolition. He was a career Army officer for 30 years and somehow has made it through every Christmas for the last 65 years.

Rifle Shot

When my big brother Bill was turning 12 he asked for a BB rifle for his birthday. He got one and he taught me how to shoot it, if I would use some of my allowance to help buy the BBs. That was okay by me. I guess I spent most of my allowance on BBs that year. When I asked for a rifle for my 12th birthday my parents agreed. I was now like the big kids. I had something dangerous. My instructions were to have fun, be safe, and don't shoot at the birds.

Since my neighborhood was mostly friendly except for an occasional short-lasting squabble that was forgotten almost as soon as it started, we never used our rifles in aggressive ways toward each other. Harold was the exception. He would sometimes shoot me in the leg and it stung so bad I'd cry. I never told anyone about it since I didn't want the other kids to think I was a crybaby.

Our main activity with our BB rifles was target shooting. We would line up sticks in the sand and shoot them down from about 50 feet away. We made targets out of cardboard and fired away at the bulls-eye. That was my favorite pastime because the BBs would get stuck in the cardboard and I could pick them out and reuse them. It was cheaper way to play. We even had our "citywide" contest that drew at least a dozen participants from as far as two blocks away. The contest was to see how many pinecones you could knock off a stump before the counter could count to twenty. The stakes were high. We played for marbles, though we never played "winner takes all."

I was the youngest among the shooters and I usually had trouble cocking my rifle fast enough to get off enough shots to score well. But I never let that get me down. When the shooting contest was over the "dirty dozen" would spin out of the wooded area where the

33

contest was held and head back to our homes. We thought we looked like an Army squad with our rifles balanced over our shoulders. I look back on the late 40's and remember those childhood days with pride. Walking around the neighborhood with a rifle in my hands made me feel stronger.

I guess I was almost 12 when Cedar Wax Wings began flying over our home in flock after flock, heading back north for the summer. They would land by the dozens in our Pecan tree and in my neighbor's Cedar tree. I went into my bedroom, got my rifle and sneaked it out the back door, making sure that Mom and Dad didn't see me. I remember thinking, since there were so many birds, that bagging one wouldn't hurt, that's for sure. I cocked and fired. No luck. I did the same many times, getting a bit frustrated after each miss. Many of the birds landed in the nearby Cedar tree. I sneaked under the tree, took aim on a big one, fired and a bird tumbled to the ground. Feeling exhilarated I stepped to the bird and picked it up. It was a Cardinal with beautiful feathers of red and black. Blood was dripping out of his left eye onto my hands. I had killed one the most treasured birds anywhere. I felt numb.

Quickly I put the bird on the ground, ran to the garage and returned with the shovel. I dug a hole under our pecan tree, laid the Cardinal in the ground, and covered it with dirt as fast as I could. When I was spreading some Pecan leaves over the burial spot to hide my deed, I thought I heard someone at our living room window. When I looked up the window was clear but the two organdy curtains were blowing separately as if someone had just been there. I didn't know. I ran back to the garage with my rifle and the shovel. I placed them both in a dark corner where no one would see them. Now what? After what seemed like an eternity I went into the house, walked into the kitchen past Mom who looked at me suspiciously, and tried to settle myself onto the bed with a book to read. All I could see on every page was a Cardinal with blood dripping from his left eye.

After supper Dad asked if I'd like to take a little walk with him. I agreed and we strolled down to the corner and back. He then suggested that we take a look at the spot where I practiced pitching under the Pecan tree. We did and he commended me for working hard to be the best that I could be. Then he slowly walked near the grave and asked what it was. I froze for a moment before coming clean. He thanked me for my honesty and reminded me of his instructions when he bought the rifle for me. I felt ashamed. Dad sent me to my room for the rifle and told me that he would keep it until he thought I had earned the right to have it back.

That happened nearly 60 years ago. At first thought it's just about boys being boys, learning to be careful not to hurt anyone. It's about being intentional to not kill any living creatures that crawl, run or fly. It also might be a stance on hunting rifles altogether, considering that hunters kill ducks, doves, geese, boar, deer, and a whole assortment of critters during every season around the globe. In spite of my childhood teaching I've made my peace with hunting. Some hunters use rifles to provide food for their tables and also to cull the number of game in certain geographical areas where overcrowding causes disease in the herds and flocks. Malnutrition becomes a problem. I'll have to admit that I still question the intelligence of a fellow who gets up at 4 AM, goes out in the woods to sit and shake on a high stand in 25 degree weather, only to hope and pray he would see something to shoot at.

I've yet to be convinced that the National Rifle Association is applying its power to influence a safer country for us all. No one really needs a vintage machine gun used in the Vietnam War. Why would anyone be allowed to own a dozen or more pistols in his home? I am concerned about gun control and how easy it is for criminals to access a pistol or an automatic weapon for the purpose of breaking the law. While supporting the constitutional right to bear arms I believe the government must find a way to require citizens to be accountable for every weapon they own or sell or pay a very costly penalty.

Perhaps the most important thought about my childhood rifle has to do with the way my Dad dealt with me when I told him the truth about killing the Cardinal that April afternoon in Orangeburg, S.C. He was quick to the point. He was forgiving. He gave me a reasonable punishment that I would remember for a lifetime.

Smelly Boots

If a dog is a man's best friend, then a dog is a boy's soul mate. Boots was my soul mate and the soul mate of my brother's too. His four-teen years with us are legendary and though he's been gone for more than fifty years we still smile whenever we mention his name. From my viewpoint Boots was our dog since before the beginning of time, though we got him as a pup when I was eight years old.

He probably was the one who gave God the idea of making cats since he never saw one he didn't chase, that is, a cat who didn't belong on our property. Strange enough, we had 18 cats, and Boots was friendly to all of them. It was those outsiders that drew his protection genes into action. Regardless, Boots was a 25-pound mix of terrier and pit bull that often ignored the terrier side of his family tree when he was outside on his security detail.

As brothers, Johnny and William and I did the enjoyable things boys do. Flying a kite was certainly among the most exciting ways to spend a spring afternoon. After buying a kite from the local "Hobby Shop" along with three balls of string that held 75 yards each we were ready for an adventure. We never did anything halfway. Following instruc-tions one day we tied the first ball of string to the kite's cross sticks, ran a short way into the north and let the south wind catch it and up she went like the hawk that often circles our home. Little by little we let out the ball of string until the kite was hanging high over the houses across the street from us. Boots just lay around in the grass pretending that he was a disinterested observer.

When the string on the first ball ran out we tied it to the string on the second ball. Immediately we had the potential of flying the highest kite in South Carolina. Two times 75 yards would be 150 yards. Slowly, very slowly we let out the second ball of string so that it wouldn't dip the kite onto the tall trees down in the woods. If that happened we would never be able to get it down. When we unwound the second ball of string we attached it to the third ball of string. We knew we could win the prize for the highest kite in the United States.

We reeled out part of the third ball and then it happened. The low hanging string that crossed our road got hit by a car, pulling the ball of string from Johnny's' hand. Down the road it rolled and bumped and bobbled at the same rate of speed the car was going. Instantly Boots jumped up and ran lickety-split after the string ball. As we watched Boots run we could also see that our prize-winning kite was taking a nosedive into the distant trees. Our prized kite was caught high in the tall pines more than a block away.

The car turned the corner pulling the string ball right behind it. Boots followed the car close behind and disappeared out of sight. We raced down the hill hoping to catch up with Boots. While we were highly disappointed over losing our kite, our spirits were quickly restored when we saw a hilarious sight coming up the street toward us. It was Boots with kite string circling around his neck and snout, wrapping over his back and under his stomach, half crippling his legs with every step he took. Boots looked like a circus animal whose task was to make the children laugh. It's been 60 years since that event but I can still see it like it was this morning.

Boots got his name because he had four white feet. I think he knew his feet gave him a real cool appearance because he would often strut around the house like English royalty. As far as he knew he was a king who deserved our best attention so we usually gave it to him. One of our favorite pastimes was dressing him in our clothes. We put socks on his four feet and our t-shirts over his head and front feet. We put our underwear upside down over his back feet so that his tail would shoot upwards through the pee hole in the front. Then we put our short pants over the underwear, which completed his royal appearance.

If it was in winter we pulled a stocking hat down over his ears. To show you what a great dog Boots was, he never whined or tried to get away from our admiration. He just stood there, looking like a model preparing for his walk down a showroom runway. We would brush his hair and pat his back with the laughter reserved for only the best comedian in town. Then we would back away and see how long it would take Boots to pull the garments off his body. He pulled the socks and the hat off easily. The short pants and the underwear came next but the t-shirt gave him trouble so we helped him with it. It would be an hour's worth of sidesplitting entertainment for us.

I didn't understand that there are distinct personalities in dogs like there are in humans. Boots was always sweet with us and nothing we did to him ever provoked him even to growl. But Boots did have a fiery, aggressive disposition that he occasionally displayed whenever another dog entered our neighborhood. He was always ready to fight to defend his territory, which he had carefully marked for anyone to smell. I also think he wanted to guard us from harm.

There was one dog that constantly crossed the territorial grounds. His name was Rick, a large Golden Retriever, owned by one of my best friends, Jay Rousseau. Rick would leave his home at the bottom of the hill, walk to the top of the hill where we lived, cross over the invisible property line and bark at Boots. That was all the challenge Boots needed. I tried to hold him back but Boot was stronger than I. Immediately his one half pit bull instinct would rush his brain and he would gallop across Carolina Avenue to the corner where Rick stood waiting for a fight. After a few seconds of circling and smelling critical points of each other's anatomy, Boots would leap at Rick's neck with a ferocious lunge. Even though he was half the size of Rick he still considered himself meaner, tougher and the likely winner of the match. The fight would scare me half to death. Sometimes it appeared that Boots won, at others it looked like Rick got the best of Boots. Regardless, Boots always came home with deep bite marks requiring a visit to the Vet for sulfur powder for his wounds. What a fighter he was. I think his medical bills were higher than mine.

Not only did Boots like to sniff other dogs but he also liked to smell the garbage truck as it rolled down Carolina Avenue. Since there were no plastic bags for garbage in the 40's and 50's everyone put all of their kitchen waste in a metal can with a top on it. So when the garbage men (sanitation workers) came to your house they would throw off the top to your can, carry it to the street, empty it into the truck, and carry the can back beside your garage. If the garbage men saw a piece of meat or fish in the truck they would toss it to Boots. Sometimes the garbage would smell awful but Boots seemed unbothered by that.

On one occasion Boots was missing for a couple of hours. We looked everywhere for him through the neighborhood. As our worry heightened the garbage truck pulled up to our home. Down came one of the men holding Boots who said that Boots had followed them all over town. Boots smelled terrible like the garbage he had been eating. We could hardly get near him. But we thanked the men on the truck and coaxed Boots to the back yard where we shampooed him several times trying to get the stench out of his hair. There was nothing we could do about his horrible breath. I think it took several days to get him back to normal, if he ever was a normal dog. One thing for sure, we loved Boots. He gave us fourteen reliable years of service and friendship.

The Victorian Guards

We called my Mother's Mom "Grandma." She had a sister named Lele. The twosome was generous to their church and often gave significant gifts to family and friends in need. Yet their self righteous, ultra religious, Bible totin' views on God and life made me curious about this thing called faith. My childhood love and respect for them hardened like a walnut shell as time went by. My early years of hugs and kisses with them turned into a revolting closeness, almost like the smell of cheap perfume. I avoided being around them and found creative escape routes to guarantee my emotional welfare.

There were the "blue" laws during my childhood in the 1940's that prohibited most stores and movie theaters from opening on Sunday but in addition there were "Grandma's Laws" that prohibited us from having any fun on Sunday. Sunday was a day of rest, according to Grandma. My brothers, John, Bill and I, had a hard time resting all day when we visited her house in Sumter, S.C. Everything was off limits. No throwing baseball or football. No running races around the house. No playing with "the Devil's" cards. Playing anything would be breaking the Ten Commandment's "Keep the Sabbath holy."

But there was an old, wind up Victrola in the garage. We would crank it up and sing songs while listening to the old 78's from the 1930's. If no one were looking, we would sneak in a swing on the old swings under the shady oak tree. But on our Sunday visits we didn't do much but complain about how good it would be to drive our 1948 Plymouth back home to Orangeburg, S.C. where playing was acceptable, if only in our backyard. Mom had a puritan streak down her back as well, only not as wide as Grandma's. We could play games on Sunday but they had to be played in the back yard so that no one would know it. I occasionally wondered if God could see us and if our play really bothered Him.

The most humiliating thing about going to Grandma's and Lele's was our last minute trip to the bathroom before climbing into the car for our trip home. Since it was their bathroom, Lele claimed the right to follow us and watch our performance to make sure we didn't mess up the floor. She would give us instructions on how to pee when I had been doing fine on my own for more than 8 years. To say that Lele, a registered nurse, was Obsessive Compulsive was a great understatement. I never wanted to go to Grandma's house for a Sunday visit. It gave me mental cramps.

My Mother became dependent on Grandma for at least two reasons. One was that Mother didn't do well at Coker College and Brenau College. Apparently her Dad spoiled her by doing too much of her homework for her during high school. As a result Mother couldn't handle the stress of college life. The second reason was that Mother was dependent on Grandma's strict requirements on dress and behavior that bordered on emotional imprisonment. Mom needed to please Grandma to keep her favor. She did at a very high cost to her health and wellbeing. Mother's personality was scissored to pattern after Grandma's. Grandma put such restraints on Mother that at times Mother's feelings were no longer her own.

My observations of Mother's behavior were best informed during my college years. After managing her life well during the 50's Mother began feeling significant depression. She was given Valium for it but it was ineffective. So in the 60's her condition worsened. When Daddy died her depression deepened. It was about that time that Grandma played the "dominator role," though she stood barely 5 feet tall. Mom got severe letters from Grandma almost daily, telling her if she had faith she wouldn't be sick or panicky. Mother would open a ten page letter critical of her dress and behavior, read a few pages and burst into tears. I was the only son at home. I knew something had to break.

I told Mother that I was going to tell Grandma that Mother was no longer going to receive any more of her letters and that I would read them first. If the letters were positive, I would give them to Mother. If not, I was going to mail them back to Grandma. Mother hesitantly agreed. I must have mailed back 25 letters to Grandma over the next several months. Then they stopped arriving. We had won the battle. Mom's self esteem returned, her depression began to lift. The Reverend Don Lannon dropped by to see Mom every day at three for at least 6 months and was a key in Mother's emotional recovery.

Mother's love for Grandma went through some major alterations. No longer did she lean on Grandma for her thoughts and ideas. Mother depended on God in a free way again, not in a constricted manner. Mother matured in her thoughts, trusted her psychiatrist, and started the long journey back to health. Over the next years she moved into the Finlay House for older retirees, then to the Presbyterian Home in Columbia where she thrived. Perhaps her years there were the healthiest years of her life. We were all so grateful and proud of Mother's new independence.

Grandma and Lele, the Victorian Guards, lived in their castle high above everyone. Their personal laws had no grace in them. They seemed oblivious to the effects of their control on others. I believe that they were unable to see how the constraints they put on Mom caused her to be a sad people-pleaser. Mom couldn't break from Grandma's chains until she was in her 60's, but when she did we saw a beautifully transformed woman.

Squeeze The Trigger

School was out for the Christmas holidays so I had been sleeping late every morning. "Get up, Robert. It's 4:30 AM," Dad whispered.

I jumped out of bed on to the cold floor. The kerosene heater that was just outside my bedroom door was dark inside. Dad said we didn't have time to light it. As Dad made the coffee and filled the thermos he instructed me, "Put on two sweaters and that long underwear, you'll be glad you did. It's 35 degrees outside."

I doubted if I needed to put on those silly looking long underwear so I'd prove Dad wrong. I put them back in the drawer. I pulled on my corduroy pants, socks and shoes, two sweaters and a stocking hat that the boys at school laughed at when I wore it during the winter months. My hand-me-down coat was too big for me but when I put it on over my two sweaters it fit okay. I grabbed my gloves that were so bulky they fit like baseball gloves.

We climbed into Dad's 1949 Plymouth and pulled out of the driveway as quietly as we could to keep from waking up Mom, Johnny and Bill. It was going to be quite an adventure for a ten year old. The only sports I played were the "big three," football, baseball and basketball. There I was heading to St. Matthews to Henry Wannamaker's farm to hunt for deer.

"Dad, why don't you take your rifle? "

"I don't own a rifle, son"

"Why not?"

"Well, my Father didn't have one either, so I never got interested in hunting."

"How did you get to know Mr. Wannamaker anyway?"

"I helped him with his taxes. Stop asking me so many questions."

"Why do parents always tell their kids to stop asking questions?" I wondered.

When we arrived at Henry's farm he invited us into his warm kitchen. There were three other men drinking coffee and telling stories of their best hunting days. Real often somebody would laugh at a fellow's story like they didn't believe it was true. But nobody laughed at Henry's stories. Maybe that was because he was the farm owner and everybody had to be nice to him. When the clock showed 5:30 A.M. Henry pulled out a big cigar, bit the end of it off with his front teeth, spit it into the garbage can with a perfect aim like he had done it 1000 times and said, "It's show time, gentlemen, let's jump in my old Ford and go down into the woods." The men placed their rifles in the trunk of the car.

All six of us packed like sardines into Henry's old Ford and slowly bumped and jostled down a rut filled road for ten minutes or so.

"There it is, gentlemen, the country palace I've been telling you about. Ain't it beautiful?"

In the headlights I couldn't see anything beautiful. We climbed out of the car, got the rifles from the trunk, and walked into the worse looking house I had ever seen. It was a one story, concrete block building. Henry lit a kerosene lamp and put it on a wooden table so that we could see one another. The door was off its hinges. The windows

45

still had glass in them but none of them could shut tightly. The cold wind whipped through the door with an eerie sound that made me nervous. Two rickety looking chairs were leaning against the wall but no one tried to sit in one.

Henry laid out a map on the table that showed where three deer stands were located. After making the assignments for the first two deer stands Henry looked at me, winked with a big smile and said, "Robert, you're with me. You're gonna bag your first deer today." It felt to me like I had just been drafted by The NY Yankees. I was going hunting with Henry!

Henry folded up the map and put it in his back pocket, picked up his rifle from the corner and said, "Robert, this is a rifle, it's very dangerous, but if you treat it right it will be your best friend."

Henry urged Dad and the other fellows to go ahead and climb into their stands but to be careful. Henry showed me how to load the rifle, to hold it and to aim it before escorting me out to our deer stand which was pretty much like the tree house in our back yard, only the deer stand was higher, maybe ten feet off the ground. Henry asked me to climb up first and then he followed. There were two small stools to sit on. A makeshift roof was above our heads but I had a feeling that if it rained, God forbid, that the roof would only slow the rain, not stop it from leaking through onto our heads.

"You like coffee, son?"

"Yes, sir, I do."

For a minute I forgot the cold. I drank the coffee with trembling hands and thought about how this must be what you have to do to be a man, get up before dark, dress up with so many clothes that you feel like a mannequin, then climb into a tree house and shoot your rifle at deer. If that's what it took, then I was becoming a man really fast.

Henry was a big man, at least twice as tall as I was and he had a Santa Claus belly that rolled out from under his too small jacket and over his belt.

"Not much room in this stand for two is there Peanut?"

"No sir," I replied.

"Well, don't try to get too comfortable anyway because this is gonna' be your lucky day, yes indeed," he whispered. "From now on we have to whisper so we don't spook the deer away."

"How do you see them? It's so dark out there."

"In fifteen minutes it'll be six o'clock and the light will be just enough to see a buck come feeding right about over there," he pointed.

"Here, let me show you how to hold the rifle and how to put it under your chin. Rest it on the board that stretches across the front of the deer stand."

Henry was so relaxed. I wish that I was steady too but the cold had penetrated my bones. My cheeks were frozen, my feet were numb and since I had to take my thick gloves off so that I could feel the trigger on the rifle, my fingers felt like ten icicles. I began to wish for my warm bed back in Orangeburg.

Yet I stayed curious about a hunter's reasoning to go through such bitter, cold weather in search for a deer to kill. If they had to go hunting then why didn't they hunt around noon when the sun could warm the day? It felt like two weeks went by before Henry spoke to me again. He began to whisper to me again in words that were hard to understand. His cigar was in the corner of his mouth and made him muffle his words.

When it turned light I could see the field just enough to tell the difference in the big trees from the little ones. Another half hour passed and the light shined enough for Henry to get excited. I didn't see with a hunter's eyes.

"There's a buck coming real slowly through the brush over there," he said quietly. "Place your rifle on the window sill, don't move, just wait"

The deer peeked ever so cautiously in front of him, took two steps, then looked left and right.

"Set your sight, Robert, and wait until I tap you on the hand before you shoot."

The buck was a tall animal with high antlers like I had seen in a magazine once. I did as I was instructed right up to the point of firing but I knew for the first time in my life that hunting was against my nature. But I knew if I could kill a deer that I would have bragging rights among my friends for a long time.

Henry tapped me on the hand. I aimed correctly and squeezed the trigger as slowly as I could. The rifle jolted me off my stool with a sound that took my breath away. Henry caught me to keep me from falling hard against the back of the stand. I peered out to see my trophy leaping like Santa's reindeer into the deep woods.

"Everybody misses their first shot, Peanut, next time you'll get a big one."

But there wasn't a next time. We waited for another try but no deer came in sight. We whispered about a lot of things for the next two hours about baseball and football and hunting.

"How many deer have you killed, Henry?" "Maybe 40 or so. I've been hunting since I was ten and I usually kill about two every year."

"What do you do with them?"

"We eat them, my family loves deer meat more than chicken. Ever eat deer meat, Peanut?"

As we waited for another chance to kill a deer we both did what men like to do and relieved ourselves from high on the stand. That was pretty much the last thing we did other than Henry unloading his rifle. Henry and I climbed down from the stand and headed for the cabin. He stopped for a moment, lighted his cigar and blew smoke into the 9 o'clock trees.

When we gathered at the cabin, Henry told the story of my miss to the other fellows. We were all invited back the next Saturday to hunt again.

One time was all I needed.

Bloody Lover's Lane

A streamlined ambulance the size of a hearse wailed its siren from at least a mile away. We dropped our baseballs and gloves and quickly hopped on our Schwinn bikes for a daring, one block race to the hospital. I guess you could say that we liked the gory side of life but we only thought of ourselves as reporters. We knew that our stories from the emergency room door would make important news for the neighborhood to hear. We were important and we knew it.

The siren got louder and louder until we had to cover our ears with our hands. When it flew past my house, screeched around the corner, and skidded to a sudden stop beside the emergency room door, the ambulance finally turned off the siren. We gathered to see someone bleeding. Any kind of blood would do. Nose blood, stomach blood, leg blood, all the same as far as we were concerned.

The doctor and nurse ran out to the ambulance to give care to the injured man who apparently fell off a ladder and broke his leg. He wasn't bleeding anywhere. My buddies and I hoped he would be okay but it was not much of a story to tell our parents and neighbors. Yes, if there was no blood, then no story. Our race to the hospital was all in vain.

Ambulances kept roaring by my house for many years and I guess I chased at least a hundred of them, but little by little my races to the emergency room decreased. I lost interest. I had witnessed every part of the human body, clothed and exposed, bloody or not, dead or alive, but at age twelve I still had a lot to learn.

I began spending more time in a wooded area near our home to take target practice with my cherished BB rifle. At least that's what I told my parents I planned to do. The truth is that there were a thousand things to do in the Woods like damming up the creek with stones and mud and picking rabbit tobacco to smoke in my corncob pipe. I thought it was cool to carve a cross in the bark of the cherry trees. Sometimes I carved SW, the initials of my secret girlfriend, in the tree just below the cross.

The Woods was known to both the children and parents on Orangeburg's north side. It was a haven for me. It was a haven for a lot of kids. One afternoon I left the sidewalk, walked past the first clump of trees and breathed in the cool air provided by the shade of at least a dozen small trees that gathered together to form a lovely canopy. Walking another fifty yards I looked upwards to the top of a monster Oak, the tallest tree in the Woods. I remembered that I had attempted twice to climb to the very top but I hadn't been tall enough to reach the last limbs at the highest point. Maybe I chickened out. I don't know, but I'm still alive. From the oak tree I walked down to the creek and crossed over it on a log my friends and I had made into a bridge. Keeping my balance was not easy and if I failed I would fall six feet down into a creek a foot deep. I settled down under my favorite Pine, thought about things, about baseball practice, chocolate cakes, my friend Jay and my secret girlfriend. The Woods was a great place for me to pull myself together.

I poured some BB's into my Red Ryder rifle, cocked it, aimed it and shot at a tree the size of a man. I cocked it and fired at a leaf floating by in the creek. When I cocked my rifle again and aimed for a pinecone, POW! A very loud shot rang out. It wasn't my rifle that made the noise. I ducked as low as I could and hugged the ground, looking for something to make sense out of the scary happening. Then I saw him lying on the ground, no more than 50 yards from me. He was screaming in pain. Was he shooting at me? If he was he was a real bad shot. The guy made agonizing sounds, the kind of sounds I had never heard before, not even at the emergency room door. Slowly the man struggled to his feet and began stumbling out of the Woods toward the sidewalk, begging for someone to help him.

I cautiously followed behind him but I was too scared to try to help him. I didn't know what to expect from him. Would he turn and shoot at me? Was he playing a terrible prank on someone he wanted to get even with? He exited the Woods onto the sidewalk and headed in the direction of the hospital a block and a half away. It was then that I realized that I was walking past his pistol, a weapon big enough to kill somebody. In moments I was stepping in a long line of blood that followed him toward the street.

By now I was seriously frightened. Should I retreat into the Woods and hide? Should I run home the back way? I quickly needed some help in managing this terrible event. Something was bad wrong. This was no prank.

I ran home the back way. Mom and Dad listened with peaked interest since they and everyone on the block had heard the gunfire. As I told my story we began to hear the voices of our neighbors. From our front door we saw the wounded man staggering up the sidewalk past our home, drenched in blood from his chest to his feet. Two neighbors, Mr. DesChamps and Mr. Martin, were assisting him as he trudged toward the hospital. Half the neighborhood made up a curious entourage so large that it could have lifted the troubled man and carried him to the emergency room. An ambulance was not needed. My family followed along, stepping over the drops of blood that trailed behind the wounded man. When the doctor met the man at the hospital door and rolled him inside on a stretcher the crowd began to pull together the bits and pieces of the happening.

The conclusion was that the miserable fellow had a girlfriend who broke up with him. He panicked. He felt cut off from the love he cherished and felt worthless. His anger boiled over. The only thing he wanted to do was to get back at his girlfriend by shooting himself. The story went that his girlfriend never did take him back again. What a waste of blood. Then again, it wasn't just my friends and me who had something to talk about that day. Now our parents had big news too.

Learning to Love

The Moving Van and the Moving Spirit

I was almost 12 when our Moving Van packed up everything and moved it from the little town of Orangeburg to the large city of Columbia,S.C. We moved into a larger home with a lot more room for everyone, including my brother, Bill, and me. Our bedroom had room for our bunk beds and a chest for our clothes. Perhaps the best part of our room was a large closet where we stored everything under the sun - shoes, Keds, baseballs, bats, gloves, a basketball, a football and two baseballs. We had a long table for our desk, one that both of us could get our feet under at the same time.

But our house and all the stuff we had still didn't give me a good feeling about moving. My mind kept floating back to my old friends and the Adden Street playground where I played sports of most every kind. And I thought about the little Presbyterian Church where the preacher was as boring as dirty socks. Somehow it was okay because it was the only church and the only preacher I had ever known. I left my heart in Orangeburg. The move just wasn't worth it.

In the summer of 1954 when I had become a teenager I had a variety of feelings. I felt everything from the pride of being the best pitcher in my league to a nagging sense of rebellion towards everything. I was angry at my parents for moving me into a town where I felt lonely. I felt ashamed over being behind in my schoolwork that occurred because the Columbia school system was better than the one in Orangeburg. I also felt ashamed about nothing I could put my mind on. Even though I attended the Shandon Presbyterian Church every week I stayed aloof from the potential power of my worship experience. As a result of my rebelliousness I hitched up with a friend of mine, Butch Askins, who lived in my neighborhood. Butch and I did have a few days of healthy activities that resulted in our being crowned as winners of the 14 and under, city doubles tennis tournament at Valley Park.

Unfortunately my rebellious nature began coming out. Butch and I picked dozens of pomegranates, rode around our neighborhood on our bikes and threw the pomegranates against many front doors that were white so that the fruit's red juice could run down them. We vandalized at least a dozen homes. My anger had boiled over. A policeman stopped us and to this day I attribute his firm, yet loving manner as the catalyst for the turnaround in my life. He required that we clean one of the porches by scrubbing it down with soap and water. My shame was intense as I crawled about on my knees, praying that I'd somehow get past this awful time. We also had to apologize to the other homeowners. The shame I felt was intense. I knew I needed some help.

The next Sunday when I went to church with my family everything looked sacred and sounded differently than before. The church was still uncomfortably large but the choir sang like angels and the congregation sang the hymns loud enough to crack the stained glass windows. Perhaps there had always been a full house every Sunday but this one was the first time I was aware that every pew was filled. I was excited to see Dr. Fred Poag enter the sanctuary. Though I had seen his entry at least 40 times before I saw him in a new light this time. Into the sanctuary he came with his long black robe with a colorful, red and black stole around his neck. He climbed the steps to the pulpit looking as energetic as a professional athlete. He struck me as someone who knew where he came from and knew exactly where he was going. His greetings were warmly cordial and his announcements informative. When he smiled his face looked like a watermelon slice, grinning from ear to ear. His eyes glistened, almost like he had shed tears just moments before. Dr. Poag's voice was the most loving voice I had ever heard, mellow and warm. I didn't think he was old enough to be bald but I respected his loss of hair as a sign of wisdom and experience.

I think it was on that Sunday, the Sunday "after Pomegranates," that I realized that Shandon Church was for me. I was ready for Dr.Poag to be my Shepherd. My awakening was happening. With my new eyes able to see the love of God I realized that I was listening to every word Dr. Poag spoke. I could hear not only his love but also his spirit of urgency for the members of the church to follow Christ and to be just and merciful in our homes, businesses, and community. He preached from written pages but he seldom referred to them because he had been serious about his sermon preparation. His messages offered a clear logic and energy that touched me every Sunday. He was like Jesus must have been for his listeners, attractive and wise, but also assertive and challenging. I was only 13 but going to church on Sundays quickly became a necessity for me. I can still feel his strong, warm hand when he greeted me when church was over. I began to feel that I could do anything, even the most difficult and sacrificial things, if I stayed by his side long enough. In my heart I made my reaffirmation of faith in Christ and felt ready for the next phase of life, whatever it would bring.

Since I played baseball all my life my model of Christianity was to be a witnessing athlete in the way that Bobby Richardson, the second baseman for the Yankees, was being. So from age 13 to 16 I continued to grow in my faith and I shared my dedication to Christ with anyone who was willing to listen. But a dramatic event happened when I was 16 years old. I went to our Presbyterian summer camp at Camp Fellowship near Greenwood, S.C. On the last night we had a candlelight worship service around a small lake. When we circled the lake Dr.

Fred Poag gave the message. We all lighted our candles. He asked for those who would like to commit themselves to full time ministry to walk around the lake and meet with him. The Holy Spirit moved me and I answered the call. I had no fear or second thoughts as I walked to meet Dr. Poag. I never had second thoughts.

The next week I met with him and the church elders to explain my sense of call. After 30 minutes of questioning the elders agreed that my call to ministry was authentic, even though candidates for ministry usually took this leap of faith in their twenties. The following month I appeared before Presbytery and was accepted as a candidate for ministry. Needless to say, my story is wrapped in the story of Christ that Dr. Poag told to me on many Sundays. He was the minister who helped me put it all together and who showed me that ministry was an admirable way to spend my life. He was the man of God I prayed I would be. Even though he moved to New Orleans during my 12th grade he continued to stay in touch with me, to encourage me, and to remind me that I was God's servant. I owe my life's vocation to Dr. Fred Poag who has been one of the primary channels of God's grace in my life.

Cheating Eyes

When I was 11 my family moved from Orangeburg to Columbia. I quickly discovered that the Columbia School System was advanced far beyond the one I had left. I was placed in Miss Grind's sixth grade class where I had missed the first six weeks of lessons. On my first day at school I learned from my new friends that Miss Grind's was nicknamed "The Amazon Woman." I'll have to admit that she looked like she could have thrown the discus or lifted weights in the Olympics. Maybe she did. Maybe she won the gold. She was taller than everybody on the faculty and sounded like Billy Goat Gruff. We could hear her walking from the other end of the hallway. At the end of my first day she walked by my desk and said, "Robert, we're having a math test tomorrow so you better study chapter 10 real hard." So I looked at my new friend, John, who sat next to me and quietly I appealed for help. He told me that he couldn't but maybe next time.

When school let out I walked home with pain in my brain and a lump in my throat. After sensing that my entire family had their own catch-up to do I settled down in my bedroom to study my math. As I thumbed through Chapters 7 through 9 I was quickly convinced that I was super challenged. If I couldn't work the math in the previous chapters how in the world was I going to perform on Chapter 10?

So when I entered the classroom the next morning and took my seat next to my new friend to be, John, my pulse rate was accelerating. Miss. Grind's walked the aisles and passed out our test papers. Almost immediately my face felt red. I knew how to work about half of the problems and that was all. The word problems were the hardest, you know, the ones where "If Jack has 99 apples and Susan has 88 persimmons and Carl has 19 watermelons, whose fruit weighed the most?" I hated that kind. Without a clue I panicked.

After all the Sunday school classes and sermons you would think I'd learned some honesty. Well, I had, but under intense pressure I unlearned it for about 20 minutes. John was a superior math student and began solving each problem like he was sliding down a sliding board. He was actually having fun with math that seemed out of the ordinary. So every time the teacher turned to write something on the black board I scanned John's paper with an Eagle's eye and plucked vital information for my score. When Miss Grind came by to pick up our test papers I just looked at my shoes so she wouldn't see my cheating eyes. I knew if I looked her in the face that she would know right away that I'd been up to something.

Immediately my heart went flat. I didn't want John to know what I'd done and for sure I hoped that my teacher would never know it. After our social studies lesson was over the class let out for recess. Since I was a fast runner I entered several races and discovered that I was the fastest boy in the school. But I found myself thinking about cheating even during the middle of a race. I just couldn't shake the guilt. After school was over I walked home quietly but there was no quiet within my soul. I decided to ask my brother Bill to help me with Chapter 10 and he worked with me until I understood all the problems. Somehow his help also helped my heart to lift a little. Yet when I lay down to sleep that night I couldn't close my eyes for a long time.

By the time I got up the next morning I felt like I'd been lifting heavy rocks all night long. My cheating eyes were playing tricks on me. I knew that I had to do something. Anything. As I walked to school the next morning I planned what I was going to say to Miss Grind but instead she spoke to me first as I entered the class. "Take your math test again and I want to watch you." The heavy rocks I'd been lifting all night were back on my shoulders again. So I began the test and managed to get them all right. My work with my brother had paid off. My teacher looked both pleased and puzzled. "Robert, you've done well, is there anything else you would like to tell me? I answered, "Can I talk with you when the class goes out to recess?"

When the classroom emptied I went to her desk and told her how sad I felt when I saw how far behind I was in math. I told her that I had copied John's paper and that I needed to tell her. She indicated that confessing my guilt was the right thing to do. "If you cheat again I'll have to call your parents in for a conference."

Well, I never cheated in my life again, other than stealing a few marbles from my brothers and a few chocolates from my Mom's Whitman Sampler box. About those thefts I had no defense. And if I was ever tempted in a big way again all I had to do was remember Miss Grind. She was no longer the Amazon Woman but a teacher who was fair and just with me. She corrected my cheating eyes.

Grace Wilbe

When I was between the ages of 13 through age 17 I had a morning paper route that was anything but routine. It was a walking route in my neighborhood of suburban homes. There were five churches within a half-mile. All the stores were on the periphery of the neighborhood. The route took me about one hour to finish, including folding my papers as I walked. Our requirement was to throw the papers on every customer's front porch so I learned to fold and throw the papers with accuracy onto their porches. I only occasionally broke a flowerpot or hit a cat that would then scamper across the banister and out of sight.

Over the years I learned a lot of lessons, such as how to manage my time and how important it was to save my money. Since I had to collect the money for each subscription by knocking on front doors in the afternoon or evening and asking for payment, I learned that some folks are always going to be late in paying their bills, even those with a new car in their driveway. Of course, there were the angels along the route too, such as Mrs. Webber who always paid her bill on time and who also offered me hot chocolate in the winter and a Ginger Ale in the summer. Some of my trips to a family's front door taught me that drinking alcohol can lead to abusive behavior and language. I saw parents screaming and hitting their children. When I would walk up the front steps unannounced I would learn from time to time memorable lessons in housekeeping, evangelical persuasion, or sex education. Perhaps my success in life came from being a "paper boy."

But there was something very strange that happened every morning around 5 AM on Wheat Street across from Saint John's Episcopal Church. When I got within ten houses from the church I could see the shadow of a woman sweeping the leaves and dirt from the street. I knew that she saw me coming her way because she began to sweep faster and faster in order to complete her task before I arrived at her home. A few houses from her home I'd see her run inside as fast as a track star. When I walked in front of her house I could easily see that all of the trash she was cleaning from the street had been deposited on her long front porch, along with all of her newspapers from 2 or three months back. It was a mess. I'll never forget the sight of her peeping at me from behind her living room curtains. Something very troubling was going on with Grace. That was her name, Grace Wilbe. I didn't know what was wrong with her but I knew that every time I knocked on her door to collect my money she would crack the door about an inch and hand me an envelope with the money in it. She was a crazy lady. She never said a word. I never saw her face.

There was one exception when the wind blew the door open about 6 inches, just enough for me to see a woman's face almost hidden inside a hood. Her eyes were dark with long lines beneath them. She had no smile. She showed no joy, only a look of fear on her face, as if my presence was threatening her safety. Handing me my money she quickly shut the door, locked it, then peeped from behind her curtain again. One afternoon after passing her home I stopped by the St. John's church to talk with the priest about my experience with Grace, his neighbor across the street. Reverend Wright told me that Grace had been acting strangely for a few years and never responded to his attempts to join him and his congregation for worship and fellowship.

A few months passed and Grace cancelled her paper subscription. I didn't see her sweeping the street anymore. She never answered the door when I would knock to inquire about her subscription. So I again went by to See Reverend Wright. He told me that Grace was depressed and had gone for recovery so that she could feel better again. One day Grace began her subscription again. When I walked up the steps to her front door Grace opened the door wide, smiled at me and said, "Thanks Robert for doing a good job delivering my paper." Grace was wearing a bright yellow dress, her black hair was fixed just right, and her eyes sparkled. I had never seen such a lovely woman. I was seeing a miracle.

Down the steps I flew and knocked on Reverend Wright's study door. When he opened his door I said, "Have you seen Grace?" He replied, "I have and isn't she beautiful?" I asked about Grace's change and how it could be. He told me, "When someone gets depressed she has something wrong with her brain that requires medicine and love to help her get well. Grace has been taking her medicine and talking about her feelings with a doctor who is helping her think in healthy ways. She's feeling good again. I've been praying for her for a long time. I know that God cares for her just like He does for us."

When I walked away from St. John's Church I waved at Grace who had her curtains pulled wide open. She waved back. I knew then that throwing papers in the early morning offered me an education that no school could teach.

Scuppernongs and Forgiveness

When I was fourteen I had an early morning paper route in my neighborhood in Columbia. I walked the route carrying a big bag full of papers that I would fold and throw onto my customers' porches. I began about 5 AM and finished around 7 AM. The winters were cold. I wore long underwear and several layers of clothing to stay warm when the temperature would drop into the teens. The hardest part of the winters was that I couldn't wear gloves since they would prevent me from folding a paper efficiently so it could be thrown to each house. My hands felt like ten icicles extending from two blocks of ice. But it was worth it because I made $20 a week that I could deposit in the bank at Five Points. Occasionally I spent a portion of my earnings on sporting goods, peg legged pants, or ice cream popsicles during recess at Hand Junior High.

But the summers were wonderful. The air was crisp and smelled like roses and honeysuckle. Birds would begin to sing around 6 o'clock before the cars hurried by, drowning out the holiness of the summer's daybreak. I took more time on my route in the summer. I didn't have to rush through the morning to get to school on time. I felt like the route was a gift to cherish. Toward August my anticipation of each morning grew. That's when Mrs. Jackson's backyard scuppernong vineyard would become ripe. Since I usually walked by Mrs. Jackson's house just before dawn I would leave the sidewalk and go into her backyard and eat some of the most delicious scuppernongs in the world. I could pop one into my mouth, bite down on the thick skin and the sweetest juice would explode into my mouth like juicy firecrackers. After eating all I wanted I'd usually pick another hand full to eat later in the day. After eating my fill I would look toward the old two-story house that was mostly dark, nothing stirring, and off I'd go to finish my paper route. It was an early morning for a King.

About the end of August the vineyard was producing the last of her annual fruit. On my last trip under the scuppernong arbor I picked the only fruit that was left. When I turned to walk from under the arbor and return to the sidewalk, for just a second, I thought I saw a shadow move in the big picture window overlooking the vineyard. I didn't think much of it at first, but the farther I walked away from the house, the more I wondered if Mrs. Jackson might have been there. Was she there? I doubted it. So I completed my route and for some reason I noticed the sunlight touching the top of my church, the Shandon Presbyterian Church. The dark color of the roof had turned golden.

The next day I began feeling like something was tight in my stomach. I ate more food, drank more milk, and pumped more push-ups than usual in my backyard. The cramps didn't go away. My mind went again to Mrs. Jackson and her vineyard. I couldn't get her off my mind. I thought to myself about the possibility that eating her scuppernongs all month long was laying guilt on me. So I planned what I would say to her if I paid her a visit. Then I jumped on my bike and instead of going directly to her home, I rode around the church a few times. When I got my courage up, I went to her front door and rang the bell. I waited for what seemed like at least an hour before the door opened wide. Mrs. Jackson was about 70 or maybe 75, I never could tell the difference in old people's ages. She had her hair pulled back in a bun. She had the same lovely smile on her face that she always had when I would come by her house each week to collect the money for her papers. I got my courage up and stammered out, "Mrs. Jackson, I've been eating your scuppernongs all month and I want to ask you to forgive me. What I did was wrong."

Mrs. Jackson said, "Robert, I know all about that. I sit at the big picture window overlooking my backyard vineyard every morning as I drink my first cup of coffee. I wait every morning to see you enjoy my grapes. I have prayed for you many times. I believed that you would eventually realize what you were doing. Now here you are. Robert, I forgave you the first day you came to my vineyard. Come in, Robert. Follow me. I want you to see where I have my first cup of coffee. It's right here at this big window. Sit down with me. Isn't it a lovely view from here?"

"Yes ma'am, it is lovely." I restated my request: "Please forgive me, Mrs. Jackson."

"You don't need to say it again, Robert," she said. "The Lord hears you the first time. He forgives you, and so do I."

And with that Mrs. Jackson pushed to me a bowl full of the last scuppernongs of the season. "These are for you."

It seemed like Communion to me.

First Date at 13

After I moved from Orangeburg to Columbia at age 11, I clearly understood that having a next door neighbor who was a 9 year-old girl was not going to please me. The property line between us was more like a wall, as far as I was concerned, and maybe it was for her too. We didn't cross over the line unless it was to retrieve a baseball or to chase an errant bubble that floated over the fence. The pre-puberty gap was naturally as wide as the Mississippi River.

But over the next 3 years our attitudes changed slightly. Occasionally I'd help Anne rake leaves in her backyard, never in the front yard because someone might see me and get the wrong impression. I didn't want anyone to think my motive revealed a deeper interest in Anne than I actually had. Sometimes I helped Anne play in the driveway with her sister, Gayle and her brother, Jim, but I believed my actions were purely deeds of helpfulness.

But by the time I was 15 I got Anne's parent's permission for me to take short trips with her to the drug store for notebook paper or to the Zesto for ice cream. These trips were always brotherly and without any romantic gesture, as far as I could assess. She was the little sister I didn't have and I enjoyed showing her the world from my mature viewpoint. She had become someone precious who needed protection. I was just the person to provide her with brotherly guidance to show her the way through the start-up of teenage life.

When Anne was 13 she invited me to escort her to her Debonairs social club dance. It was our first real date. It was the grand opportunity for me to proudly show the town my little protégé' so I accepted her invitation. On dance night I drove our family's 1954 black Plymouth around to her front curb, walked to the door in my tuxedo, one that

I had purchased a couple of years before because I was attending so many formals that it was less expensive to buy one than to rent one. When Anne came to the door in her long formal gown she had been transformed. No longer was she the little girl next door. For a moment I remember being speechless over her looks. I think I must have said some awkward things at that point, some stuttering things that sounded more elementary than the cool guy I usually was around both guys and girls.

But when we got in my car I settled back down, got myself together, and remembered that she was almost a child. My job that evening was to present her formally to the public, to show everyone how lovely she was. I cleared my mind of emotional interference in order to assure her success. When we arrived at the Wade Hampton Hotel ballroom the band played the first slow song, I placed my right hand on her waist and held her right hand with my left. I don't know who taught this Baptist girl to dance but she placed her left hand on my shoulder and we moved to the rhythm just slightly. She followed my lead. On purpose I looked over her shoulder at the other couples dancing and must have talked about how nice everyone looked. Then she said something, I have no idea what it was and when I looked into her eyes I hoped she didn't see my confusion. Was I Anne's protector or her date? I didn't know the answer but I distinctly remember pulling her a little closer to me. I couldn't believe that I wanted to get closer to this woman-child but my instinct pulled me into a surprising submission.

Before the first dance was over she seemed suddenly familiar. We had grown close in a friendly way over the last few years but this was different and I knew it. Our backyard talks, our raking leaves together, our caring for Gayle and Jim together, our trips to the Zesto, they all had been adding up into something unintentionally powerful. I remember doing my best to camouflage my internal feelings and my external flustering over this ambivalent situation. Without a thought I pulled Anne close enough to be cheek to cheek, not in love style but in dance style. By the time the band finished the first song it might as well have been the last song. I was confused. There I was, the big man on campus in high school, in total disarray over a 13-year-old, junior high girl. I hoped other dance partners weren't looking at me.

Anne and I talked with friends during the next song that was a fast one. I was strangely moved to dance with Anne again. I think she was as ready as I was. So when the next slow song began we walked to the dance floor only to find ourselves in the middle of at least 25 couples. Everybody was looking at us, or it seemed that way to me. I don't know why I pulled her closer to me than before but when our cheeks met again I felt a quiet rush like a hot wind of the Spirit that I would feel for years to come. Only moments passed before I felt something move within me, something God gave me. That was the first time I knew that I was in trouble, how serious I didn't know.

Through the evening we made small talk with a variety of couples. We talked about teachers, sports and parents mostly. But little by little I began to compliment Anne on her dress and hair and beautiful eyes that sparkled. She returned her compliments to me. Eventually I told her how pretty she looked. I was saying things that I never intended to say. What was I thinking? I'm supposed to limit myself to being her guide into social life but there I was talking like there was something more to come when the dance was over. I felt foolish, like I had given more of myself than I expected.

On the way home Anne sat a little closer to me than where she sat on the way to the dance. That seemed natural because we had been close on the dance floor all evening. Neither of us said anything about it. Our conversation was limited. Since we didn't need to talk we just sat quietly most of the time while listening to Perry Como sing "Some Enchanted Evening" or hearing James Brown scream out "Old Kind Of Rock And Roll". I didn't park the car in front of her house. Instead I parked the car in our back yard. I did the right thing and opened the door for her to get out. We opened the gate that separated my home from hers, leaving it open, which became a symbol of our future lives.

We talked in a whisper so that we wouldn't wake up her parents who were asleep in the bedroom that overlooked the back porch. Somehow I believed that they might be gladly watching our every move. We climbed the narrow steps to the top of the porch. Anne unlocked the back door and turned to say or do something, what I'll never know. All I do know is that when she turned to face me she had a look that will forever be mine to cherish. Our eyes met and I leaned over to lightly kiss her lips that were prepared for the moment. It was a lightning bolt that shocked my senses. All I could think to do was to hurriedly say good night.

That sweet peck was to gently say thanks for the evening but it foreshadowed loving expressions that would last a lifetime. It was a kiss of love, hope and wonder.

Hot Garage

Anne and I were steady dates during much of our high school and college years. Since we lived next door to each other I had the option of picking her up in two different ways for a date. Sometimes I would knock at her front door and walk her to my car waiting at the curb out front. That was usually reserved for formal occasions like parties and proms. But usually I walked out of my back door and over to hers to get my date. We would walk together to my garage, hop in my black 1955 Plymouth, back out and drive away to a movie.

Sometimes we would go inside to a movie, though I have to admit that going to a drive-in movie offered me the chance to get a lot closer to Anne which was a major priority for me, and I think for her too. Cold weather didn't dampen our spirits either. Drive-in movies gave us the chance to snuggle up under a warm blanket during winter. During summer times we did find the mosquitoes annoying but we always used our stash of mosquito coils to smoke away the pesky things. I think we spent more money on mosquito coils than we did on popcorn and cokes, but that was okay since it helped us meet our first priority of snuggling close.

The truth is that even if we went to an inside theater we still wanted to hug and kiss before the night was over. So after a hot dog and milkshake at the Zesto in Five Points, we would drive up the big hill to Heyward Street, turn in at 2524 and creep as quietly as we possibly could into the right side of my two car garage. When I turned the lights off my Plymouth the world would go black, except for the shine on Anne's ivories that gave me a hint about how to extend my arm around her shoulders. My Dad's 1958 Buick was in the left side of the garage. When our eyes adjusted to the darkness we could see the outline of his car and also our faces up close, not that we needed to see anything at all. It was a mysteriously wonderful place to be. We would slip down low in the seat, hug and kiss, and talk about the future. We would talk about college, about marriage and how many children we wanted to have. Sometimes we would talk about our family life and how fortunate we were to be loved.

One late, winter evening we made our way home from a movie and drove into the garage, settled in for some delicious tasting lips, and we heard the back door of my house open and then shut. It was about 10:30 pm and both of my parents were normally asleep at that hour. Who could it be? I looked over the front seat and in the half moonlight I could see the outline of my Dad. He was standing on the back steps motionless. I whispered to Anne to be quiet and still until he went back inside the house. We weren't really afraid of my Dad. He was gentle and soft- spoken. He was even shy unless he knew you well. After 5 minutes or so he stepped down onto the grassy lawn and paused there for just a moment and began walking toward his car. I have to admit that my heart raced a bit and this time it wasn't because I had Anne in my arms. I quickly began to think how I could explain my way out of the situation if Dad caught us there. We weren't doing anything wrong. It wasn't like I needed to hide my behavior. It was just that we didn't want anyone to view the magic we shared.

Quietly we whispered to one another the things that we might say to Dad to explain why we had the windows so fogged up in the Plymouth. Both of us had ideas I'm sure, such as "we just pulled into the garage a minute ago and we were just getting out." But we didn't have time to come up with any other excuses because in my rear view mirror I could see Dad walking in our direction. Anne and I slipped down a little lower in the front seat. Our heads were barely above the seat level. There we were, young innocent lovers, delighting in the festivities of darkness, wondering what would become of us if Dad strongly disapproved of our place of courtship. Would he expose our hideaway to Anne's Dad too?

Our imaginations roamed wide and wild. The drama heightened when Dad entered his side of the garage and made his way to the driver's side of the Buick and opened the door. The overhead light in the Buick turned on. We feared the worse was about to happen. Dad could have seen us crouched down together if he looked to his right. We were only 8 feet apart. Dad sat down in his seat and reached his right arm down to the box of Kools under the front seat. He pulled out a pack, tapped it against the dashboard to pack the cigarettes tighter and opened the pack. He was in no hurry. Dad never was. His idea of exercise was a snail paced stroll with Mom one block to the Methodist Church and back. Eventually he stepped out of the car and closed the door. Now that the car light was off I could barely see him standing by his car. Anne and I felt slightly relieved and breathed for the first time in minutes. What would he do next? Call out our names and request that we exit our valuable dating zone? Would he say nothing to us and then ask Anne's Dad for a meeting of our minds? With the flash of his cigarette lighter Dad was smoking a Kool cigarette. We could see the red tip of his cigarette light up and his face along with it. His lighter distinctly clicked shut, a click that we heard in our home for years, a sound that reminded us that Dad was nearby.

It was a night that we wished Dad would have gone to bed early instead of playing the role of sentry over his household. He left the garage slowly with the coughing sound of a man who smoked two packs a day. He disappeared momentarily behind a center petition on the front side of the garage. Anne and I took a deep breath with gratitude that we were apparently escaping the unknowns of the evening. No such luck. Dad reappeared in my rear view mirror. He was standing 5 feet behind the car looking at the moon. I don't know how many drags you can get from one cigarette, maybe 10 or 15, but I'm certain Dad got at least 100. It seemed that he would never finish his smoke.

What was he thinking? One thing for sure, he loved Anne. He told me that I ought to marry Anne when she and I grew up. I think he knew a lot that I didn't think he knew. I think the worse that could have happened that night would be for Dad to suggest that we do our courting in the house. But there was Dad blowing smoke our way. If he stayed much longer we would have to come out of our hiding place in order to get Anne in by her curfew. We were running it close. It was a situation where I might have to choose to get in trouble with my Dad or Anne's Dad or both.

Almost like he had been stargazing and knew exactly what time it was, he slowly turned and walked back into the house. Our breathing got normal again but it took at least five minutes. We slowly and quietly unfolded ourselves from the front seat and walked across the back lawn with our heads up high like there was nothing unusual about the evening. When I reached the back door of Anne's home we lingered only momentarily. We shared another kiss and said goodnight.

Our close call with Dad was never mentioned to me. Anne's Dad never said a word either. Somehow I think Dad knew we were in the Plymouth in the dark and came to remind us that young lovers need to carefully chaperone themselves in a hot garage in spring. Maybe he knew something we didn't.

Christmas Party at the S&S

As far as I can remember, I've been religious. My memory of faith in God goes back to age 7 or 8 when I lived in Orangeburg, S.C. At home, at church and with kids in my neighborhood I remember having a welcoming attitude to a Holy Presence. I couldn't articulate specifically just who that presence was, but I knew before I could read the Bible that Jesus was someone I wanted to listen to, to talk with. He was authentic from my beginning. My relationship with Him didn't keep my mind and behavior from trouble but I was amenable to constant spiritual adjustment. Thankfully there were key people all around me to guide me "in paths of righteousness for his name's sake."

One of those adults was Jim Reynolds who was my next door neighbor in Columbia, S.C. Jim was as active Baptist deacon, married, father of three, one who would become my bride in the not too distant future. When I was in my early teens Jim took an interest in me. He asked for the score of my baseball games and for a report on my grades to make sure I was balancing my responsibilities. Maybe the most interesting questions he asked were about my church and youth fellowship activities. Jim even casually quizzed me on what the Sunday sermon was about and what it meant to me. I never felt uncomfortable or defensive under his loving examination. He always made me feel that he was on my side and asked these questions only to make me think about my faith.

Around Thanksgiving when I was 16 Jim invited me to speak to his Sunday School Christmas Party at the S & S Cafeteria on Sumter Street. He said that he thought the 60 or so class members would like to hear what a young Christian had to say to them. I swallowed like a pelican swallows a spot tail bass and accepted his invitation. The big lump in my throat lasted a couple of days until I began to gather myself and develop some helpful material to incorporate into my speech. I chose a couple of parables and tossed in some quotes from Longfellow, Thoreau, and at least one from Samuel Johnson, one that I remember even today, "Great works are performed, not by strength but by perseverance." Somehow my speech wasn't coming together so I took notes from a printed sermon Billy Graham had preached. I organized my material and laid my speech aside for a few weeks. I picked it up again a couple days before the Christmas Party just to make minor changes if needed.

Help! It looked about like a guitar with no strings. Panic! So over the next couple of days I made the speech look fresh again. I was ready. When I arrived at the party, I was invited to sit at the head table, my first head table! When the plate of baked chicken and green peas arrived my shaking hands informed me that I needed to pull myself together. I couldn't keep the peas on my fork long enough to get them into my mouth. Lord, what have you gotten me into now? I wished I was home playing Monopoly with my brothers or singing carols around the piano with my Mother. But there I was, facing 60 adults all decked out in red and green and looking like they wanted me to give them some food for thought. So after Jim introduced me with several accolades, I found myself at the podium with the toughest task of my life. I think I said the first sentence twice and followed that up by claiming that a quote from The Psalms was from Joshua. I couldn't follow my notes. I was in trouble!

That's when it happened. I looked up at the class and felt the need to leave my notes. I made eye contact with a few of the class members, then panned the audience and decided to give my personal testimony. Since I was a newcomer to the Speech Circuit I found that telling

78

how God had been working in my life was preferable to a "cut and dried" presentation. As I was relaxing my shoulders and my voice I could tell that the class was listening with interest. It was marvelous. I spoke for about 30 minutes and felt like I could have answered questions for a long time too. When a nice round of applause was given to me I felt something I had never felt before. I had trusted God for the task and I had been rewarded for my efforts.

That evening played a larger than life influence on my years to come. Six months later I felt called to ministry while attending a summer youth camp. My church's elders agreed that I was on the right path. A month later my Presbytery gave me their blessing also. I was on my way to USC and Columbia Theological Seminary in Decatur, Georgia. I was ordained in 1967 in Jacksonville, Florida.

My neighbor, Jim Reynolds, who became my Father when I married his daughter Anne, played a giant role of spiritual mentor in my family life and in my ministry.

Pabst Blue Ribbon

It's hard to be good when you're 15, especially when your friend has a brand new Desoto. Well, it wasn't really Jason's Desoto, it was his Mama's, but on the day of our baseball games he got to drive it to the ballpark. Jason left his house around12:30 PM for our 5 PM game at the best ball park in South Carolina. Slick was his first pick-up and rode shotgun, then Jack who lived just up the street by the high school climbed in the back seat. I was the last man on board and sat in the back with Jack.

When all four of us were on board Jason would proudly say, "Hold on to your hats, boys," then he would push the "push button drive" on the dashboard, "pop a wheelie" and away we would go. You see, in the year 1958 Desoto came out with a "first." It was the first car to have its gear shifts as pushbuttons located just left of the radio. And I think it was also the last year for the innovation. Too many motorists tried to find a new radio station but accidentally pushed the reverse button while the car was moving. Needless to say, the transmission would grind to a metal chewing, ruin in the middle of the road.

But there we were, flying around our Shandon neighborhood, even into Eau Claire across town, all dressed up in our uniforms that read "Post 6" across the front. Maybe the proudest thing about us was our cleats. We could walk from the car across the sidewalk into the little grocery store on Divine Street and make the coolest sounds, a clickety-click sound of our baseball shoes that let everybody know that we were the coolest guys in town. When we got into the store I would buy the Milky Ways and the bubble gum because I was the shortest guy. Jason would buy the Lucky Strikes and the boiled peanuts because he was about 6 feet tall and looked old enough to smoke.

Then Jack would come to the counter last and buy the Pabst Blue Ribbon beer since he was about 6 feet 3 inches tall and showing off a beard. Slick usually stayed in the car reading a science book while we stocked up on candy and sin for the afternoon pre-game show. Slick thought we were wasting our time when we could be learning something in our spare time. We all climbed back into the Desoto and off we would go.

Picking up chicks was never a problem for us. We were "good looking, rich, drove fast cars, owned houses in Miami, Nassau, Paris, and New York." At least we thought of ourselves that way when we dressed out in our uniforms. With bubble gum, boiled peanuts and beer we were ready for the world. It seems to me that we picked up the same three girls before every game. The drive to pick up the Eau Claire girls was worth our time and the cost of gas. They were pretty, laughed a lot, had hot lips, and didn't talk around much, which was important you know, since a bad reputation might hurt our chances of getting a contract with the Yankees or the Dodgers. So we scooped up the girls, drove to the baseball field and parked under the tall, Live Oak, just beyond the centerfield fence, around 400 feet from home plate.

The oak tree was high on a hill and from our car we could see the entire field. We could see the coaches and the other players arriving around 3 PM. That gave me about 2 hours for blowing some super bubbles that would occasionally plaster my face. It also gave me ample time for some fooling around. Jason enjoyed his Lucky Strikes and a Pabst Blue Ribbon. He was known to do a little fooling around too. Jack inhaled a few Luckies, woofed down a bag of boiled peanuts, casually drank a Pabst Blue Ribbon or two and, of course, did his duty to enjoy the ladies. Occasionally we were halfway serious about our amorous advances but most of the time we laughed ourselves silly about a joke or a story somebody told about our great baseball days.

For good measure we all tossed in a few stories of our romantic conquests. As for Slick, he got out of the car, sat down on the ground and leaned up against the closest oak tree with a science book that made him feel right at home. Occasionally he would come over to the car and steal another Milky Way.

For the lucky girls, well, they got to hang out with some heavy hitters and that's all they seemed to want in life. They knew that we were literally good swingers and that turned them on, or so we thought. Somehow those three girls resisted our hormonal surges to a large degree, which prevented my buddies and me from pre-mature fatherhood. I think the boys and also the girls knew that we all were safer in numbers.

When the coaches walked onto the field at 4 o'clock we, the "Live Oak Lovers," peeled out of the car, tucked in our shirts, slipped our cleats back on, kissed the girls one more time and off we headed to the field. I swaggered like a bull-riding cowboy, amazed over how marvelously strong a woman can make a man feel. Jason walked onto the field smelling like a pool hall. And Jack walked to the mound to throw batting practice with the help of Richard, our catcher. His Pabst Blue Ribbon usually had not worn off. Now that's not funny, then again there is something funny about everything, if we put our minds to it. Jack was a fireballing pitcher. When the game started he could throw that rock faster than anybody we knew. So when he wobbled up onto the mound and looked at the batter standing in the box, look out! Jack was unbeatable through his first four innings. He terrified every batter because he threw so many wild pitches around the batters' heads. By the fifth inning Jack's Pabst Blue Ribbon had worn off and he became just "another pitcher," nothing to write home about.

It's funny how life goes. Our coach, Sammie, was once a knuckleballer for the Red Sox before wiping out as an alcoholic. But he put his life back together and his mentoring put Jack on a dry mound. Jack never made it to the Yankees but he did get a scholarship to college. Thank God all of us made it out of the "Live Oak Lovers" parking days without a new baby for the dugout. Jack and I are still happily married to our high school sweethearts. I don't know about Jason but I heard he was a tobacco farmer down around Goose Creek. I have a hunch he's still driving his Mama's Desoto. It still drives good memories. Slick teaches science in his hometown high school and coaches baseball in the spring. As for me, I've been a preacher all my life.

My Main Love And Maine

My life's direction was beginning to circle back on me. I was a 19-year-old rising junior at USC and my girl friend, Brownie Allen, and I had mutually agreed that our 2-year relationship had been wonderful but was now only a friendship. That's not the way it was supposed to be. We had planned our wedding in her home church in Georgia, decided on the seminary I would attend in Atlanta, and believed that 2 children would be about right for our family. Since she was already an accomplished organist it would be easy for her to get a job as the organist and choir director in a church nearby. It was all planned out. It was so good. But when our romance went from seeing each other every 2 weeks to every 5 or 6 weeks, we decided to let each other go free to seek the person God would bring to us in time.

I guess it shouldn't surprise me that for a couple of months before Brownie and I broke up, I had restarted conversations with Anne Reynolds, my high school sweetheart. I had to respect Anne's feelings and go slowly because when I broke up with her 2 years before it was painfully disappointing. I knew that if we became close again it had to be once and for all. I wasn't sure of myself. To give me time to think about it I decided to leave town for a while. Around May 20 of 1962 I applied for a position in Maine at the Colony Hotel. In my application I claimed that I was about the best in everything that they might need at The Colony. I wanted so much to be out of town for a while that I probably sounded like Superman in order to attract the employer's attention. It worked. George Banta called me within a few days and offered me a job. He wanted me in Maine on May 25 to start work. Excitement hardly defines what I felt that day. It was a mixture of pride, courage and anxiety. I got a job with a hotel manager who didn't know me. I was prepared for an unknown adventure. What was it going to be like to live in Maine, our northernmost state?

I packed my suitcase and jumped on a train at 9 A.M. heading to Boston on May 24th. My imagination reeled with scenes of surf pounding against rocky shores, lobster fishermen lifting giant lobsters from their traps, and artists painting colorful pictures of fishing boats entering the harbor. Arriving in New York I could feel a biting cold on my neck as I changed trains for Boston. In Boston I stepped down from the train and my entire body shivered from the wind. I walked a block to the bus station, bought a ticket for points north, and sat for 3 hours in what must have been an experiment to see whose feet froze first. When my bus was called I gladly jumped on board first to get the best seat possible. It was about 10 PM. I got the front seat so that I could see the highway. What I saw shocked me. An hour out of Boston I saw snowflakes falling. The bus windshield wipers swiped away the snow but it got heavier as we made our trip north. I was glad I was in a warm bus only 2 hours from Kennebunkport, Maine. What about the snow? I'd never seen snow before. It was lovely but I didn't bring winter clothes with me. I needed boots, a warm coat and a stocking hat. What had I gotten myself into?

The bus pulled up to a crossroad and screeched to stop in three inches of virgin snow. A sign off to the right read, "Kennebunkport 3 miles." It was midnight. The bus door opened and the bus driver pointed to the sign. When I inquired why he wasn't taking me there he simply told me that the bus line only went to the crossroads, not down to the port. I thanked him, picked up my suitcase, and stepped down in the snow. As the bus roared away I looked around at what was surely a winter wilderness. I had come a thousand miles. How was I going to make the last 3 miles to the hotel?

I was relieved to see a small country store and walked in to get out of the cold. The potbellied stove had a faint glow, the wood almost burned out, so I knew the owner of the store was about to close up. I explained my predicament and the owner said The Colony Hotel, which was to be my employer, was shut tight and wasn't scheduled to open until June the 20th. He noticed my slight despair and offered to phone Edwin, the security guard, to figure how to solve my problem. Edwin said he would pick me up within 30 minutes if his car would start. If not, he wanted me to walk the 3 miles in the snow to the hotel.

I was grateful to the store owner for his help. A half hour later Edwin's car rolled up beside the store. I put my suitcase in the backseat and climbed up front with Edwin. He was a scruffy-looking fellow, maybe 60 years old, and looked like he had been to sea more than a few times. He didn't say much, only that I would stay in his house for a week or so until he cut the heat on in the hotel's staff quarters. When I climbed into a spare bed at Edwin's I wished for the pair of long johns that I occasionally wore back in Columbia when I'd deliver papers in my neighborhood. It must have been 50 degrees in my bedroom. I got out of bed and quickly put my clothes back on before climbing into bed for the second time. I was disillusioned with my introduction to Maine.

The next day George Banta, the hotel manager, called me at 7 A.M. and asked me to meet him at the hotel at 8 A.M. I trudged through five inches of snow to the office and met a man who was all business. After a ten-minute conversation during which I verified that I could do most anything well, Mr. Banta said that he had about a hundred letters that needed to be typed and mailed by the end of the week. I accepted the challenge and mailed the letters on time.

During the next week he taught me how to be a desk clerk, a bellman, a waiter, and a kitchen assistant. The snow melted in the middle of June and George taught me how to keep the large putting green that was in front of the hotel. George said he needed me to be the guy who could fill in whenever an employee got sick or couldn't perform their duties for some reason. He even taught me how to clean the swimming pool and barkeep, even though I was only 19 and not allowed behind the bar. I was well prepared when the rest of the 40 employees arrived at the end of June.

With a great surprise I learned that 25 of the summer staff for the hotel were college students like me. Most of them were from Northeastern schools like Yale, Boston University, Penn State and NYU, and there were a few from Michigan and Ohio. As the only Southerner I was daily ribbed about my drawl. I must have said, "Hi Ya'll" a thousand times and reaped the same hilarity each time. I ribbed back at their Yankee accents too.

We stayed in a dorm facility with all the guys in one large room and all the girls in one next door. The rooms were somewhat like you would expect to find on an army base, just a little more comfortable. Over the summer we became close as a team. Some of us enjoyably paired off. My date was a lovely girl from Michigan, Diane Ducharme, a junior in college like me. She was a devout Catholic and I was a serious pre-ministerial student so we had similar values that grounded our conversation and behavior.

There were so many stories to tell. My income was the greatest story of all. In Columbia I was making $400 a month. At The Colony I had a base income of $400 a month but with opportunities for tips throughout the day. When I was bellhopping, I could often get another $400 a month. Doubling my income at the hotel meant that I could pay my way through USC for another year.

Through the summer Anne and I wrote to each other only occasionally. We cautiously examined our past, wondering if the break-up I caused two years earlier had left too much scar tissue for reconciliation to occur.

After three fabulous months at The Colony, two of my friends and I resigned so that we could take a vacation before we went back to school. Frank from Yale, Dale from Penn State and I drove in Frank's car from Maine through Vermont and New Hampshire over and around the most beautiful hills I'd ever seen. We drove through customs at the New York border crossing and made our way to Montreal.

After three days of sleeping late, seeing the city, riding a cruise boat down the St. Lawrence, and eating delicious meals, we wanted to see the countryside. Our destination was the fir forests where few people lived. Three hours north of the city we were surrounded by nothing but trees. There were no more houses or stores. When the paved roads ended we drove on dirt roads for a while until we saw a sign in front of a building that read "Sisters of Charity." We were hungry and decided to knock on the front door. A mature woman in her 60's in her habit welcomed us in. We shared that we were hungry and several sisters fed us a meal of soup and the best bread I had ever eaten. In a spirit of thanksgiving and after a deep conversation on faith and religion, we traveled back to Montreal for some more delicious cuisine.

It was time to go home. Shakespeare, Herman Melville and Abraham Lincoln were waiting on me. Frank drove Dale and me to Boston where we caught trains for home. I was a very proud man jumping down from the train on that early September day in Columbia. Approaching my house I felt ambivalent. I was excited but a little anxious too. I wondered if three months away from Anne would open our hearts to love each other again. I got out of the car and walked toward my back door. I saw Anne at hers. I put down my suitcase and walked through the gate that swung between her house and mine.

The Dawn's Early Light

Late one Sunday afternoon I had a few hours break from my work at the Colony Hotel in Kennebunkport, Maine. I walked down to the harbor like I often did to watch the fishermen dock their boats and unload their catch for the day. There were two trawlers whose fishermen appeared satisfied with their day's work. The boat captains engaged playfully in the "mine's bigger than yours' game" to see who had the best haul of the day. Their laughter told the real story. Each of the crews had done right well and would be rewarded for their day's hard labor.

I had been reluctant to speak to anyone. Perhaps it was because I didn't know the first thing about fishing and might get caught sounding foolish if somebody asked me a question or two. I didn't know the names of the fish they were bringing out of the hold and I didn't know how the trawlers worked their nets. I kept my distance and observed the harbor's activity. But each week I noticed a man making new lobster traps and repairing some old ones. I walked within about 30 feet of him. He was dressed in a short sleeve, red t-shirt with grubby looking black pants. His black knee high boots were so tight they looked like it might take two people to help him pull them on and off. He sat Indian-style working on a trap and without looking up he adjusted his baseball cap and asked,

"I bet you're one of those city boys working up at The Colony aren't you?

"Yes sir, I am"

"Bet you're going to college too. Which one, Yale?"

"No sir, South Carolina, didn't have enough money or brains to go to the Ivy League schools."

"I got my education right here on this dock," the man explained. "Been learning in this Fish School for almost 30 years now"

He leaned on the trap he was repairing and glanced up at me with soft and easy eyes and calmly said, "You ever eat lobster up at the hotel?" "Yeah, whenever the chef boils more than are ordered. The staff gets to share them."

"I trapped-em. I've got a contract with the hotel to supply 'em, usually 25 a night."

"How many do you catch every day?"

"35 or 40 on a good day. You like fishing, you want to check traps one morning with me? It would be an early rise and shine for a college boy, we shove off at 6, back at 8 o'clock"

"I'll have to get a substitute to pinch hit for me at the hotel but I can do that. I'm a good swimmer if necessary. You wear life jackets?"

"Nobody gets in my boat without one. How about Monday morning?"

"My name is Robert," and I extended my hand toward him that he pretended not to see. He never looked up and with assurance said, "Mitchell, when I've known somebody a long time they call me Mitch."

For the next hour Mitchell showed me his traps and how they worked. He explained that he had 15 traps within a mile of the harbor and that he always rotated 3 of them for repair because the salt water was hard on them. One broken trap meant a loss of good income. I was surprised at Mitchell's quick offer to carry me out with him to check his traps. I was even more surprised that I accepted his invitation. I had been with him only a few minutes and now I had committed to going the next day with an unknown man whose life I knew almost nothing about. Was he a safe person to be with? Was I putting myself in harm's way? I had no way of knowing. He could be a man of faith like I was or he could be a guy accustomed to growling at God through his own disappointments in life. Was he safe on the water or would I be paralyzed with fear as he went from trap to trap collecting his lobsters? I had overnight to think about it.

When I finished my shift as the desk clerk at the hotel it was about midnight. Since I had to get up at 5:30 A.M. I went right to bed but I didn't fall asleep before 2:00 A.M. I couldn't get off my mind the thought that my normally good judge of character might not be so good this time. Perhaps I should show up but give Mitchell an excuse about having to work a shift for one of my buddies who got sick in the night. That would fly. Mitchell would never know.

The Monday morning clock rang off. I dressed and walked quickly to the dock. All the way down the street I rehearsed my lines. I had them memorized and felt ready to play my part in the charade. In the dawn's early light I could barely see Mitchell standing in his small boat, apparently waiting on me. When he saw me he whistled and said, "Come on Jake." I thought he had forgotten my name until a brown mutt came running from the boat house and leaped into the boat." The closer I got to the boat the more I knew that I couldn't tell Mitchell a lie.

"Ease into the boat, Bob, step into the middle of it. We don't need to capsize before the sun comes up good."

When I eased into the boat it was clear to me that the only seat available was the one Jake was sitting on. I sat down next to the shaggy 40pound dog with hair falling down over most of his eyes. One thing for sure, his coat kept him from feeling the brisk morning air that was now settling on me.

"Does Jake always lick everybody's face like this? I'm getting a real bath down here."

"Nope, just people he likes. He makes friends quickly if he thinks they're safe to be around." Mitchell pulled his pipe from his teeth, emptied the dying embers into the bottom of the boat and said, "Untie that rope by your head and let's shove off, we don't want to keep the crayfish waiting."

Mitchell pulled the engine cord to start us up. The oil and gas exhaust fumes from the engine drifted over to Jake and me. I was momentarily asphyxiated but Jake obviously knew to hold his breath till the blue smoke drifted by. We motored slowly out of the harbor past the trawlers whose crews were readying their boats for the day's trip into deep waters. The crewmembers and Mitchell waved with the sign of the cross without saying a word. I laid the meaning of the signs into the back of my mind and concentrated on our trip. The dawn's earliest light began putting a glow on Mitchell's face. He looked momentarily at my face for the first time, probably because morning was shining on me too. As quickly as he looked my way he looked away again. I wanted to ask him what he had seen when he glanced my way but something told me to keep my mind on lobsters.

"C'mon, Jake, cut it out, give me a break."

"Is my dog bothering you, Bob?

"Yeah, he licks me in the mouth every time I'm not on guard. It wouldn't be so bad if his breath didn't smell like garbage"

"Jake does like his garbage. He sometimes looks like a grizzly, tearing into fish the fellows on the trawlers throw to him."

"You're right about that, Mitchell, his breath is something awful. Where'd you get Jake?'

"He strayed onto the dock ten years ago. He looked emaciated so I fed him some lobster meat, that's all I had. I'm embarrassed to say but that's all he eats now. Jake's the best fed dog in town. He goes wherever I go and he's got good manners except when he likes somebody and feels safe."

We motored in front of the hotel about 200 feet from the shore. As we passed a couple of traps I reminded Mitchell what I was seeing. I asked him if there were no lobsters in those traps and he nodded his head to the front and back. I was a true rookie. I didn't have a clue about what was going on. After a thirty minute trip from the dock past the hotel and a few spectacular homes we reached trap #15. Mitchell explained that to keep the lobsters fresh he takes them from trap #15 first, then #14, until he had gathered them from all fifteen traps. "It keeps them fresher that way," Mitchell said.

I quietly said, "Sounds like the first shall be last and the last shall be first. It's something in the Bible."

"I don't think much about preaching," Mitchell said. "It don't make a lot of sense to me. Too confusing for me. Do you know much about the Bible, son?"

Cautiously I said, "I'm learning bit by bit, but I've got a long way to go"

"To go where? You're not gonna be a preacher are you? Lucky me, I've gotta preacher in the boat with me."

His tone was mildly sarcastic. Maybe he was trying to avoid talking about something he was struggling with.

"I didn't mean to offend you, Mitchell. Everybody's got a right to believe the way they want to."

Mitchell's voice trailed off, "It's a long story, too long to tell."

We stopped at a few more traps and emptied them into the boat. We had about 20 lobsters and we were half way home. So far it was a good day according to Mitchell. I enjoyed watching him unlock each trap, reach down into it, and bring out each lobster with the loving precision that a Father does when he picks up his baby out of the crib. Every time Mitchell pulled another lobster from the trap Jake barked with pride.

Suddenly the sunrise was darkened by the light fog that was rolling in which made for an eerie scene. Our visibility was instantly limited. We couldn't see the shore, nor could we see the harbor a quarter mile away. In the distance the trawler's engines cranked up. It was almost 7 o'clock and they were running late getting away from the docks. As the boats made their way out of the harbor Mitchell emptied another trap and put it back into the salt water. He cut his engine for some reason and listened intently. Mitchell knew the harbor and the ocean channel probably better than anyone on the coast. What was he listening to?

"Something's not right. One of the trawlers is off course. Now I can see her coming, but we're too small for her to see us yet."

"What's the matter, Mitchell?"

"She's coming too close to us and there is gonna be a high wake. Steady yourself. Hold on to both sides of my boat because it's gonna rock big time."

"How about Jake?

"Aw, he's alright, he never falls out."

When the trawler passed us there was a long silence before I saw the wake slowly making its way to our small boat. It was taller than I thought it would be. I braced myself without any consideration that I was in any danger. The wake hit our boat, we rocked landside, then seaside, and when it tipped back to landside I went over the side like I was in a diving competition. When I surfaced Mitchell extended me an oar and pulled me to the boat.

"Hey Bob, you alright? I told you it was coming. Aren't you glad we wear life jackets? Some people don't and they make their home at the bottom of the sea."

"Yeah, the wake was bigger than I thought it was."

"Climb in. Move over Jake. You know, falling out of a boat can be really dangerous. I don't want to lose two Roberts."

As I kicked my knee over the side of the boat and took my seat next to Jake who obliged me by trying to lick me dry, I said to Mitchell, "What did you say about losing two Roberts?"

"Nothing. I just said that we need to get you dry, so let's rob these traps and get you back to the dock."

"I'm okay, just shaking a little."

We returned to the dock and unloaded the lobsters. We walked silently together during our one block trip to the hotel. Mitchell carried a large box of lobsters and headed for the hotel kitchen. I headed for the shower.

I didn't return to the dock to see Mitchell for a few days. My sense of it was that Mitchell was walking a tight rope above something important to him and that I ought to leave well enough alone. It was like Mitchell had a painful pearl cloistered in his heart that no one was allowed to see. Before the week was out I found myself praying for him, hoping that he would be glad to have me back at the dock again. In spite of the dredging I took when I went overboard I still believed Mitchell and I had something going for each other. He was a fascinating man and I wanted to know him better. He reminded me a little of my Dad. When I got off work on Wednesday it was about noon. I decided to wade into the murky waters of relationships to see how I'd be received. At the dock Mitchell was crouched over a lobster trap like a baseball catcher trapping a low pitch.

"What was your catch like today, Mitchell?"

"Not too bad, coulda been worse. Crayfish are spending too much time courtin' to climb into my traps."

"Did you deliver them to the hotel already?"

"I did. Gotta get them there by 11 or the Pope will buy somebody else's crayfish."

"What do mean, 'The Pope'? There's no Pope around here."

"Oh yes there is. Tall Ed Sloop, the chef, wears the tall hat and runs the show. What he says goes. He's The Pope," grumbled Mitchell.

I agreed, "Well, when you think about him like that, I guess you're right. At The Colony, Pope Sloop makes the rules, interprets the rules, and carries them out also."

Mitchell came back with, "My church, that is, it used to be my church, trapped me once. It took a long time to get out. I had to give it up."

For the second time in our brief relationship I could tell that I was unintentionally fishing for information that might separate us. I didn't want that to happen. I wanted to slow down the terribly fast pace of Mitchell's disclosure. I had spent only a little more than three hours with him and most of the conversation was about lobsters, not about us. So I sat down on the dock with my feet hanging over the side and watched minnows darting under and around Mitchell's boat.

Changing the subject I casually said, "Tell me about the trawlers that come and go from here? You know them well?"

"Yeah, the captain of the 'Fish Tales' has been on that boat for almost forty years, twenty-five as captain. Thomas has seen it all, been through it all. "

Without sensing the direction of the conversation I said, "I bet he's seen sunny days and stormy days in his time."

A silence split apart our talk for what seemed like an hour before Jake showed up to bathe my face with his eyes. I didn't know what was coming next but it was Mitchell's turn to go. I waited.

"My son was twenty when he decided to leave college and become a fisherman. Since I'm a fisherman and make my living on the water I had little ground to stand on when I told him to finish his education before deciding on a career. He made up his mind and left the University of Maine where he was an "A" student. After interviewing with Thomas on board 'Fish Tales' he enjoyed two adventurous years and saved most of his money. He wanted to take a trip around the United States one summer."

I could feel it coming. I swallowed hard but I kept my eyes on Mitchell's lips that trembled ever so lightly.

"Ten years ago a storm hit the Northeast and the 'Fish Tales' got caught fifteen miles off shore. Thomas, the captain, asked the crew to bring up the nets and come inside. As the crew worked together a wave poured over the stern and swept Robert, my son, away. He wasn't wearing his life vest. The cardinal sin for fisherman to be on deck without one,"

I was speechless. As naturally caring as I was I still couldn't open my mouth. So I waited, hoping God would provide me with something to say to a father who still grieved his lost son after ten years. When he finally spoke Mitchell said, "I think I'm totally over it and then I see a young man like you and a wave hits me again. My son's name was Robert."

I felt like an emotional dam had broken. I maintained my silence for at least five minutes, not because I didn't have anything to say but because his story was sacred and deserved holy time. He needed to let it rest in his heart again. I gave him the time he needed. When I did speak I said, "I'm sorry Mitchell, real sorry."

With his eyes comfortably resting on mine he said, "Just call me Mitch."

Football Fools

You would think that my USC friends and I would have plenty to do without adding another extra curricula activity to our schedule. But classes and labs, homework, part time work and, of course, gorgeous girls were just the beginning of our interests. When we got a little bored our minds shifted to playing tricks on each other in the dorms and fraternity houses. We poured water on sleeping students. We lit paper in a trashcan and hollered "fire" in our fraternity house. One of the most rewarding tricks was tying several sheets together and tossing them to girls on the dorm's second floor, making a rope ladder for us to climb into the girls' rooms. Today the girls and boys dorms are open for visits anytime.

But we pulled our ultimate trick on our archrival, the Clemson Tigers, in Carolina Stadium in late November, 1962. It was designed to be a humorous humiliation of the Tigers during the warm ups of the Carolina vs. Clemson football game. Our Sigma Nu fraternity found a high school, which had the same orange and purple uniform colors as Clemson's. The high school coach was a University of South Carolina grad and agreed to help us pull off the trick. He would do anything to get Clemson's goat.

On game day the coach brought us his team's equipment under the Carolina stands. We dressed in Clemson colors, pants, shirts, shoulder pads and helmets. Many of us wore our loafers and other kinds of dress shoes just to accentuate the ridicule of Clemson's fans. So after planning our entrance on to the field we decided to do the routine, ridiculous "warm ups" and exercises that we knew would make the best fun of the Tigers. Our goal as Clemson imposters was to get the Carolina fans in stitches while getting the Clemson fans embarrassed and infuriated. We informed the Highway Patrolmen in our area what was about to happen. They were getting a kick out of the trick too and promised to stay out of sight for as long as possible.

Our team hit the field knowing the potential for a fight. It was no time for the meek. Our big guys wore undersized jerseys and our little players wore the biggest jerseys. Not one player looked like his uniform fit. Neither the Carolina nor the Clemson fans realized right away that they were seeing a sports masquerade. As planned we ran routine practice drills that we had practiced the day before. Our linemen stumbled and fell over each other. Our quarterback threw wobbly passes to receivers who let the balls smack into their faces causing them to fall backwards. Our kicker practiced punting the ball backwards over his head. The Carolina fans realized what was happening first and roared with laughter. I don't think there was any beer left in their cups. After our placekicker practiced his kickoffs, totally missing the football, he would upend himself as if he had slipped on ice.

That was the moment of reality for the Clemson fans. They poured onto the field, maybe 200 of them. Obviously we had touched a sensitive nerve. We who were impostors tried to get off the field before a fight broke out. Half of us did. I was in the group that got caught on the field. The Clemson fans wanted to make a feast of us. They hit us with their fists but they only got bruised knuckles since we were wearing our helmets. A few of us like me got wrestled to the turf and rolled around without injury. By then our Carolina fans ran on to the field and for the next five minutes there were some punches thrown but most of all there was a lot of shoving and bragging. Dozens of South Carolina troopers broke into the crowd of about 400 warning they would arrest all students who continued to fight.

The crowd split. Clemson fans went across the field to their seats. Our

Carolina fans went to theirs. As we left the field, we got a standing ovation. Undeniably, our masquerade was the greatest in the history of the school. We've talked to a lot of alumni over the years, and we have yet to find a trick to beat ours.

Turn Your Eyes

In 1956 I attended a summer camp, Camp Longridge, for a week of fun, flirting with the girls and playing softball. We stuffed down meals that were almost indigestible, went to Bible Study and Evening Vespers. The Evening Vespers were led by a country preacher who knew his Bible like I know the back of my hand. And we always sang his favorite hymn to close the worship. It wasn't "Jesus Loves Me" because that would be too childlike for a group of 14-year-olds who were trying to act like we were 21. Neither was it "A Mighty Fortress Is Our God" because it would be over our heads and too heavy for kids who were growing up listening to Fats Domino and Bo Diddly. Instead we all sang, "Turn Your Eyes Upon Jesus," written by Helen Lemmel.

One night when I climbed into my top bunk in our cabin and our talking began to simmer down to silence, I could still hear in my mind the tune to "Turn Your Eyes Upon Jesus." I couldn't remember the lyrics because when we were singing the closing hymn out in the amphitheater my eyes were clearly upon Eve.

As the week progressed I enjoyed the camp experience more and more. But at the strangest times I'd catch myself humming the beautiful tune in the shower, the dining hall or on second base playing softball. The tune became an escort for Eve and me as we walked by the lake and talked about things 14 year-olds talk about when we're afraid to talk about love. The tune and eventually the lyrics just became a wonderful part of me. It strangely pushed out of my mind most of the unkind thoughts that go along with being human.

I kept up with Eve off and on over the next year and then we fizzled out like a roman candle. But what didn't fizzle out was my love for the wonderful hymn. It stayed with me through college and seminary.

When I returned to the camp during my seminary days as the director in 1965 and 1966, I taught it to about 1200 youth and children. Maybe those kids are still singing it too.

Thirty-five years later when I resigned from my pastorate in Raleigh due to illness, the congregation sang "Turn Your Eyes Upon Jesus" the last Sunday I was in worship. When Anne and I moved to Columbia we attended the Trinity Church on our first Sunday in town. The choir sang "Turn Your Eyes Upon Jesus." On the next Sunday we attended Shandon Presbyterian Church and the choir sang it.

As difficult as it was to move to a new home, when the beautiful hymn was sung three weeks in a row in three different churches we knew that we were still in the same spiritual home with God.

"Turn your Eyes upon Jesus

Look full in His wonderful face

And the cares of earth grow strangely dim

In the light of His glory and grace."

Changing Times

Harmonizing With My Soccer Coach

In the summer of 1960 I fell in love with the girl that I believed would be my wife one day. I began my first year at Presbyterian College in Clinton, South Carolina, and Brownie Allen enrolled at Queen's College, a Presbyterian college for women in Charlotte, North Carolina. Since I didn't have a car I caught a ride or thumbed my way to Charlotte as frequently as possible. Any way was a good way. In hindsight all my weekend trips that included skipping classes on Saturdays may have slightly lowered my GPA. Back then I didn't want to admit it. Love won out over education.

But there are a couple of parallel stories. When the door opened for me to go to Presbyterian College I was elated, partially due to the joy over being accepted at a good institution with a Christian foundation. I had committed myself to become a minister and P.C. was the right place for me. The other reason for my excitement was that I had been offered a partial scholarship to play baseball and run track in the spring.

Life at P.C. was good. I pledged the Sigma Nu fraternity and met guys that I felt comfortable with from all around the South. But my time with my fraternity brothers was limited since I was leaving every weekend for Charlotte to visit Brownie. In addition, I worked in the dining hall 15 hours a week to cover my room and board. So my main friendships developed in the dining hall and kitchen. My best friend was Lindsay Odom. Lindsay loved to sing as much as I did. We and our other workmates were a fraternity of our own. We called ourselves the "WPFJ" or "Washing Pots For Jesus" guys. Our best song included the lines, "Oh, P.C.'s trying to grease us, so we're washing pots for Jesus." We sang songs we knew and also made up songs of our own. Sometimes as we sang half of the diners would sing along with us. It was a hot and greasy job in the kitchen but I think those hours were the best hours I had on campus.

My friend, Lindsay, played half back on the football team but after a leg injury that slowed him down he left the team. One day in November he asked if a dozen guys and I would meet him on the football practice field. We gathered together, mostly burnt out football jocks and a few spring sports guys like me. Lindsay told us that the USC soccer team wanted us to come and play them a match. None of us had soccer in our vocabulary. What was it? He took a ball from under his arm and bounced it on the grass. It was larger than a softball and volleyball, but smaller than a basketball. USC had given us the ball with the challenge to play them on Saturday. Well, it was Friday so we had only one afternoon to learn the game. Lindsay taught us the game that he had learned on Thursday. No matter how hard he tried to show us that the game was not like football, somehow it didn't register that this was a finesse game, not one that required macho muscle.

On Saturday our team, if you could call us that, jumped into a few cars and drove to USC. It was time to test our athletic experiment. I'll never forget walking onto the field that was between the old gymnasium and the Russell House on Green Street. We were the only Anglo dudes on the field. All of the USC players had international faces that were Asian, Middle Eastern and South American. Since integration had not begun there were no African students on USC's team. Even though we were wearing old, faded football jerseys we certainly didn't need to wear them to tell our players from USC's. Since they all looked small, more like me than the rest of our burly looking team, right away our hopes climbed quickly. We could take these fellows!

The whistle blew and the game was on. USC players kicked and passed the ball back and forth and between us like we were statues on the field. USC scored its first goal in a matter of seconds. Their players could move the ball around with the precision that our basketball team could pass and dribble the ball. Our PC players tried hard but our brawn was no match for the agility and plan of the USC team. We did win in one way. We injured more of their players through our rough playing. We didn't mean to run into those guys but we just weren't used to playing the game by the soccer rules. At the half the score was 6 to O. As the game wound down we were exhausted. They had hardly broken a sweat. The score was USC 11 PC 1. We were humbled. Driving back to campus in Clinton we agreed not to tell our friends how badly we had lost to USC, but when we entered the dining hall wearing our faded football jerseys the students were inquisitive. When we told them that we had played USC in an afternoon "soccer" game many students asked, "What's a soccer game?"

The next weekend our soccer team decided that it would visit the nearby Newberry College but it wasn't to play soccer. Newberry was our arch rival in all sports and we loved to play tricks on each other, not just during football season but most anytime. At about midnight on Friday before PC was to play Newberry our "team" of 12 crammed into two cars, along with 2 gallons of gas and drove the 15 miles to their football field. We parked our car near other cars so that we wouldn't call attention to ourselves. Two by two we walked onto the football field with our gas can. With our adrenalin at peak level a couple of our guys poured the gas on the midfield grass in giant letters, "PC," probably 10 feet high from top to bottom. The rest of us kept a watch out for any Newberry students. We lighted the letters on the field, made sure that they were beginning to burn and ran as fast as we could to the football field exit.

Two by two we quickly walked back to our cars. Newberry students walked pass us on the way back to our cars but we kept our heads down and crammed back into our cars. As we drove away we could see the faint glow of our dirty deed through the gaps in the stands. We slowly made our way off campus without notice. We did it! We pulled off the ultimate trick. Going to the game the next day to see the game being played on the burned letters of "PC" at midfield was a winning day, even though we lost the football game by a huge margin.

My enjoyment of Presbyterian College abruptly ended. The school board decided to discontinue giving scholarships for spring sports. My half scholarship to play baseball and run track was no longer valid. That decision swept me down a sad river. Without my scholarship aid I didn't have the necessary funds to stay at PC. When the semester was over, I said goodbye to my friends, especially to Lindsay. I moved out of the dorm and traveled back to Columbia to enroll at USC. Lindsay and I made plans to get together during the summer. His Dad had a boat and we talked about going skiing together at Lake Murray. But in early June Lindsay drowned in the lake.

No Sweat

It was a scorching hot day in August of 1965 when Anne and I were married. In the sanctuary there were 999 candles burning up and down the aisle, across the podium, throughout the choir loft, then down again to the floor level where Dr. Jerry Hammet and Dr. Enoch Brown were waiting by the Communion Table to perform the ceremony. When I walked into the room with my brother Bill, who was my best man, I could easily see that the sanctuary was running over with family and guests, sitting shoulder to shoulder in an almost uncomfortable way. I couldn't tell by their faces who was Baptist, Presbyterian or Methodist but I knew there was a of representation of most denominations on that blistering Saturday night in the Shandon Baptist Church on Woodrow Street. I think that at least half of Columbia was in attendance.

My tuxedo was soaked by the time I saw my lovely bride, Anne, at the back of the sanctuary with her Dad, a man I'd learned to respect for his faith and his fatherhood. My mind wandered momentarily to the memory of my cousin who passed out and fell to the floor during his August wedding ceremony in Bishopville a few years back. He had to be propped up by three groomsmen who continued saying to him, "Say I do, Emsley, just say I do, say I do." On our wedding day things looked like I might need to eye a place for me to sit on the first row, just in case. The bright lights and heat from all the candles in the church were either showing the glory of God or warning us of the fires of hell and I didn't really know which one it was. All I knew was that I wanted to shift our holy time into high gear before I succumbed to the rapidly rising temperature.

The bridesmaids and the groomsmen, all 12 of them, looked like firefighters ready to run for the fire extinguishers to rescue the congregation from certain danger. They, along with the two ministers and my brother Bill, safely passed by me on their way to their designated placement for the ceremony. I could feel their love for Anne and me as they all gathered around us in a tight semicircle. I also could feel their heat, which added to my rising discomfort.

It seemed to me it took Anne 45 minutes to walk from the back pew to the front of the church where she joined me and the two ministers who said some spiritual things about marriage and love, but for the life of me I couldn't tell you what any of those things were. I just kept looking over at Anne who was the most beautiful creature on God's good earth. I was thinking, "I sure hope they get around to the "I do" part before one of us hits the carpet like a sack of potatoes."

The temperature when the wedding began was maybe 85. By the time we got to the rings ceremony it was probably 95 degrees. The congregation politely mopped their brows. The wedding party inconspicuously moved their wet forefingers across their foreheads, hoping the congregation wouldn't think that their movements distracted too much attention away from the bride and groom. I could feel the sweat running down my sideburns like a mountain creek after a summer rain. The preachers, robed in traditional black garments, looked like they had just walked in from a late afternoon drizzle. But the miracle of the day was that Anne looked cool as a cucumber. Her hair was perfectly combed and her veil seemed to have sheltered her from the heat. Her neckline was just as I had loved it so many times over our 10-year courtship, beautiful beyond words.

Finally the preachers read the part where we exchange rings. When my brother Bill reached into his pocket to get Anne's ring out, he couldn't find it, or he said he couldn't. To this day I don't know whether he could or not, all I know is that when he finally found it, my hands were so wet and trembling that I could hardly stabilize them long enough to slip Anne's ring on her finger. Then she easily pushed my ring on my shaky finger, which of course slipped on like it had been lathered in cooking oil.

While the benediction was being said, I kept thinking, "If we can get through this wedding, we can get through most anything, for better or for worse, in sickness and health." When Anne and I walked back up the long aisle we were amazed to discover that it was hotter in the church than it was outside. As we made our way on the sidewalk around the sanctuary to the fellowship hall we agreed that one thing for sure, we were going to get married just once. We've both lived by that decision to this day.

However, God only knows that both of us have sweated through times of trouble, big time trouble. Our union has been threatened by storms in most every decade, storms that were created primarily by my unhealthy dedication to the church and a slow, simmering mental illness. At times my churches fared better than our marriage did. Fortunately Anne understood more about the dangerous floods that can tear a marriage apart than I did. During my most serious illness, my bipolar disorder that has changed the way we live, Anne knew that there was sunshine above the threatening clouds, even when all I could see was a flood that was washing away my dreams.

God has seen us through yesterday and today. The future will be the same. God has shown me several colors of the rainbow. I believe He will show me the rest of the colors in time. I'm trying to be patient, knowing that my ways are not God's ways. For me it isn't easy. But as Anne's Dad used to say about God's ability to love us through our dark days, "It's no sweat."

Mother-in-Law

It had been a long but wonderful day when Anne gave birth to our son Mark in St. Vincent's Hospital in Jacksonville, Florida. Everything had gone perfectly. Both Mother and child had escaped any trauma and were resting easy. I knew that everything would surely continue to go perfectly when Anne and Mark came home the next day because we had mapped out just how we would handle everything. We had planned for groceries and meals, though we would soon find out that the women of the Lakewood Presbyterian Church were going to joyfully feed us every day for a week. Since I was the Associate Minister at Lakewood Church I knew that the women would go out of their way to meet our every need.

The best part of our plan was to invite Anne's Mom, Evelyn, to come from Columbia, S.C. to stay with us for a week or so to help with the many tasks that needed to be done when a new baby comes home. Since Anne and I grew up next door to each other I had grown accustomed to talking with her mom on many occasions, sometimes routinely and at times with deeper spiritual meaning. I looked forward to her visit with us for a week, so on the Saturday that I drove Anne and Mark home from the hospital there was Anne's Mom, a welcomed sight, standing on the front porch, ready for duty.

I don't know just how she did it. Evelyn changed diapers, washed diapers, washed our clothes and sheets, vacuumed the floors, and managed the meals as they arrived. She was a whirlwind of accomplishments and Lord knows, her work made it possible for me to enjoy my growing family. The first morning at home was a breeze, there were so many things to do but Evelyn and I divided up the chores. She did the hard chores like the washing and vacuuming, while I did the easy ones like holding Mark in my arms and rocking him like I was a pro. Anne changed Mark's diapers and breast-fed him by the clock. Anne was tempted to get up and help with the house chores but in 1968 a new mother was told to stay in the bed for a lot longer than new moms are told today. So she spent most of her first day at home in the bed with Mark in her arms. Thanks to Anne's mom our plan was working like a charm.

At the end of the first day at home I was exhausted from excitement. Anne was exhausted from childbirth, Mark was lying peacefully in his crib, and Evelyn was wiped out from all of her housework. So I encouraged Evelyn to go with me to our second bedroom, we only had two, where I reminded her which single bed was the most comfortable and she agreed with my choice, the one next to the window. I pulled the blinds shut and expressed my deep gratitude for her service. She smiled and told me that this had been a wonderful day for her with the arrival of her first grandson. We also agreed that not even the afternoon and evening rains could put a damper on such an occasion. After saying good night I closed the door. We had done it. Nothing could go wrong from here.

I slept with one eye open that Saturday night, so glad that Anne could be getting needed rest. But we both took turns checking on Mark, listening to his breathing, marveling over the miracle that he was. Around 3 A.M. the rain got heavier and so did my eyes. I was afraid that if I closed my eyes that I might fall asleep at just the time Mark needed to be changed or fed so I sat on the side of the bed looking thankfully into the crib. What a child! To this day I think his feet were dancing to the rhythm of the heavy rains. What a child!

Crash! The sound came from Evelyn's room! Was someone breaking into the house? I leaped to my feet, shot to the door of Evelyn's room, and immediately realized I was standing in a shallow stream flowing under her door. By then I could hear sounds of distress from Evelyn's room that included, "Robert, what have you done to me, help?" I quickly opened her door and a wall of water rushed past me and I would have fallen if I hadn't grabbed hold of the door frame to steady my slippery steps. I cut on the bedroom light and to my shock I found Anne's mom looking more like the devil than the angel that she truly was. Not only was her lovely brunette hair now soaked with rainwater but it also had been straightened with a combination of plaster from the ceiling and small roofing rocks that had rushed down through the roof onto her bed. Her soaked nightgown was literally plastered against her body revealing her body's small frame. It was then that I was shocked that I was standing before my mother-in-law in nothing but my underwear. Out of modesty and the threat of electrocution I immediately cut off the light, leaving us groping in the dark for a guide. I did have my wits about me long enough to suggest that she grab a dry nightgown from a corner chest. From there I led Anne's mom through the water to the living room and gave her a couple of dry towels and a sofa to sleep on.

Thankfully the rain suddenly stopped. We agreed that both of us should get dry and try to fix the flood when the sun came up and we could see what to do next. The sun rose around 6 A.M. and Anne couldn't believe what had happened over night. She and Mark had slept like babies through all the calamity of a Florida storm. Her Mom and I reassured her that we would take care of the damage and have the house back in order before the women of the church arrived with our lunch. We both tackled the inside, mopping and squeezing for what seemed hours. I called into the church to let them know I would be in a little late. That gave me time to repair the roof. The ceiling would have to wait. About 9 A.M. I leaned the ladder against the side of the roof, carried up a broom and a 5 gallon bucket of tar and began sweeping the rocks away from the source of the leak. When the rocks had been cleared away I poured the bucket full of tar in the cracks of the roof and swept the rocks back on the tar to make the tar bond. Done!

Down the ladder and into our bedroom I hurried to dress for Sunday church service. It was a proud day for a father of a new baby boy and I didn't want to miss the handshakes and congratulations from the congregation. I stopped long enough to kiss Anne and Mark. When I got to the living room I wondered what Anne's mom would say or do. She opened her arms and told me how proud of me she was. I don't know what I preached on that Sunday. If it wasn't on Jonah and the whale it should have been.

There are dozens of jokes and complaints that men offer about their mother-in-laws that demean their character. Mine is a different story. Evelyn literally braved the storm without complaint. Over the years her service was always helpful, never intrusive. As sure as she was an angel to us she is definitely an angel in heaven.

Lost In The Pulpit

I had a humble cockiness about me during my seminary days, probably because I could spend so many hours making money for tuition and still do well academically. It was difficult but I made A's and B's in most classes with occasional C's in Hebrew. As hard as I tried I could never make much sense out of the Hebrew alphabet. When we were nearing graduation all of my classmates and I had the privilege of having conversations with churches seeking a new minister. Somehow I got the opportunity to talk with two of the most sought after positions available. The first was a church on Signal Mountain, Tennessee, a wealthy congregation rather segregated from the rest of Chattanooga. The people were genuine but very wealthy and right away Anne and I knew it wasn't the one for us. Our second opportunity was a suburban church in Jacksonville, Florida. When Anne and I paid a visit to the Lakewood Church, we immediately fell in love with the people and I believed I could work well as the Associate Minister with the Senior Minister, Charlie Benz.

We bought our first home, which was big enough to turn around in and small enough to conceive our children in. At church we made good friends, with George and Anne Smith and Jack and Jo Varney, who welcomed us into their lives and played wonderful roles in youth ministry with me. I quickly learned a lot from Charlie about administration, counseling, and officer development. I also found Charlie to be a very solid preacher who did his homework and always delivered a powerful message. After worship I would often take notes on his preaching style and content.

In my first year at Lakewood in 1967 I preached every four or five weeks. I think I could have preached more often but in hindsight

117

that schedule gave me time to prepare my next sermon well. Charlie preached from handwritten notes. I typed mine since that was the way I was taught in seminary. The first few sermons I remember to be well developed and strong, normally three typed pages. I always developed a clear, easy-to-follow outline before I wrote my sermon in detail so that it would flow naturally for the congregation to hear. When I delivered my sermons I always felt confident so I looked up from my written paper frequently to establish good eye contact with the people.

One Sunday morning I climbed into the pulpit with my Bible and preaching notes, excited and ready to go. After reading the scripture, which I remember to this day "In Christ the old has passed away and the new has come," I placed my Bible to the side and began to preach from my three pages of notes. I knew it was one of my best because I felt inspired and several members of the church began to nod their heads up and down. Finishing page one I slipped it aside only to find page three. Where was page two? I looked about my seat and on the floor, but no page two to be found. I panicked for a moment but it didn't take me long to remember what page two was all about. So I stepped down from the pulpit, moved in front of the communion table, cleared my throat and began to speak as if I had planned it this way all along. The longer I preached the more energized I felt. People were listening intently and smiling. The congregation and I were experiencing a new day.

I had crested a high hill and could see a new horizon for my preaching style. From that day forward I only developed a detailed sermon outline that I would occasionally use if I felt a bit unsure of how to move into my next point. But I poured my soul into the outline to make sure that it was totally logical in every sequence. That made it easy for me to preach by visualizing the outline, which I kept in my Bible in case my mind was distracted in some way.

I believe my preaching style was effective over the years. I think it contributed to the spiritual well-being of my congregations and strengthened their commitment to service. Years later at Saint Andrews in Raleigh I taught this style to all my associates who learned to appreciate its value in their own ministry. It's ironic that my carelessness in 1967 helped me become a more effective preacher. That change in preaching style humbled me. I never felt cocky again from that time forward, but I took inspiration from that preaching experience. Good things can happen from things that trip us up. I've been helped all through my life by keeping my eyes on what God can bring out of trouble.

Stormy Sail To Nassau

Maybe it's because I get bored with things as they are and want to do something new that gets my mind working on ways to accomplish a new goal. I suppose that's why I looked at our church's camping program and thought it would be great to offer a new experience for kids in Florida. I began contacting sail boat owners and captains in Miami to see if we could work out a high school camping (sailing) week to Bimini and Nassau in the Bahamas. I contracted with Captain John Lucas to sail us on a beautiful 52-foot ketch christened "Safe Passage." I was the first mate, though I had little experience in sailing. When we needed to raise and lower the sails, John said he would briefly put me at the wheel and he'd work with some of the kids to make sure that everything was set right. The kids were going to be in charge of food preparation. It sounded exciting. I had no way of knowing just how exciting it was to be.

So on a Sunday morning in July of 1971 we motored out of Miami Harbor with sixteen high school kids, Captain John and me. We all waved goodbye to the parents standing on the dock who waved goodbye to us with a prayerful look on their faces. The kids' joyous anticipation was trumped only by my own.

We unfurled the sails about two miles out of the harbor when the wind was strong enough to move us along. John gave me and three kids the directions to accomplish the task, and in spite of it being our first attempt to set sails we did okay. John cut the diesel engine, and everything went silent for a moment. I asked all the kids to come on deck and gather together in a tight circle near the wheel. I reminded them of the great privilege we had in making the trip, one that few will ever have. My next request was that each youth tell something about themselves and to tell it loud enough for Captain John to hear it. After a half hour of storytelling I asked that they all be quiet for ten minutes and listen to the wind, to the Spirit, to God. After the quiet time had ended I asked the kids if they heard anything and if they would like to share anything with the group. It was interesting how many thankful and meaningful contributions were made by the kids after being with one another for less than an hour. I've always believed that silence is as important in spiritual growth as verbal teaching is.

On our 45-mile crossing to Bimini we naturally gathered on deck or below in two's and three's for conversation. I stayed close by Captain John to learn as much about the ship and the ocean as I could. After three hours sailing, the crew enjoyed sandwiches for lunch made by the kids. When lunch was over, Captain John suggested that we drop anchor, put on life vests and jump into the sea for a short swim. Half of us did and it was a welcomed relief from the hot sun. We climbed back on board and within a few hours we were motoring into the crystal clear waters of Bimini. We were glad we had made reservations because the small harbor was filled with boats, mostly large and small fishing boats that people would charter for half day and all day trips.

We docked our boat and began to explore the island. Renting small motorbikes was the favorite pastime. Walking the two-mile island was fun too. I knew that drinking alcohol was not prohibited for any age, so the kids could walk into a bar and order whatever they wanted. My warning to them was that I would fly them home if they got into trouble. None of the kids disappointed me. Perhaps the most exciting part of being in Bimini was watching the fishing boats dock and unload the most beautiful fish we had ever seen, We saw swordfish, tarpon, 100 pound grouper, and also 6 and 7 foot sharks. We also had great fun shelling and swimming on the beautiful beach. Our two nights on Bimini were so good that the kids wanted to stay for one more.

But they had a treat coming to them that wasn't on their schedule. So on late Tuesday morning we set sail for Honeymoon Island, an uninhabited playground for both kids and adults. We surprised the kids when we sailed into Honeymoon's waters and announced that this was our harbor for the next two days. It was one of the most alluring places in the world with unspoiled, white sandy beaches, lovely shells, shallow water, waves that were safe for everyone, Palm trees for shade, and soft sand for lying out for tans.

It was temporarily great for everyone. But as night fell, there was some grumbling about nothing to do, no interesting fishing boats to see, no motorbikes to ride, and no lights anywhere. There wasn't anything to do! Of course, that was the point of going to Honeymoon Island. I wanted the kids to experience life without commodities and to understand that life is good when it is simple. At the end of the second day the youth were growing to love each other and were beginning to learn the important spiritual lesson that I was teaching.

I didn't know what I expected a long sailing day to feel like but our seven-hour Thursday trip was to be our longest. We sailed from Honeymoon Island mid morning, headed north past Bimini, then headed east towards Nassau, the largest city in the Bahamas. Captain John checked the weather and though there was a storm to the south he decided it wouldn't affect our voyage. This leg of the trip was more troubling however, since the sea waves rolled more than on previous days. Many of the kids were seasick and couldn't keep their food down. Sometimes they made it to the commode in time. On other occasions the clean-up crew was quite busy. I felt like I was going to toss my cookies too but I just stayed on deck where I encouraged the kids to stay.

We lowered our sails to have more control of the boat and Captain

John cranked up the diesel. Captain John began a zigzag course to manage the southern wind that blew harder than the weatherman had predicted. By 4 o'clock the seas kicked up a mist that sprayed across our faces. Low clouds blocked out the sun. I looked at John and he showed concern but when I asked him if we were okay he smiled back with a wrinkled brow.

We figured that we should have been in the harbor in Nassau before nightfall but we were at least an hour away from safety. When the rained started around 7 P.M. our visibility shortened to about 200 feet. When a heavy line of rain hit us our visibility was even less. Around 8 P.M. I was wondering if Jesus was going to walk on the water to us like he did to his disciples on Galilee. On the other hand, I wondered if our boat was soon going to be on the bottom of the restless Atlantic. I've never been a pessimist but our situation was beginning to look dangerous.

Captain John told all the kids to put on their life vests and go below in case a wave hit the deck, He told me to put my vest on, go forward, to sit down on the deck and wrap myself around the forward mast with my legs and arms in case a wave should break across the bow. He asked me to keep a lookout and let him know if I saw anything. If I did I was to holler loudly and point to what I saw. Since we were at least an hour from Nassau I figured he meant something like a lighthouse or another sailboat, lost at sea like us. So I did as ordered. Clinging for my life, I would hear John hollering for an update on what I saw. I shouted at least a dozen times that I had nothing to report. Then I thought that I saw something. It was my imagination for sure, just my fear in a blustery storm.

Suddenly, from my left I saw moving lights in long rows. I wiped away the rain from my eyes and blinked a few times. It couldn't be.

I hollered to Captain John and pointed across the bow in frantic motions. What was it? Whatever it was, it took Captain John only a couple of seconds to spin the wheel starboard (right) as far as it would go. The lights on the strange night vessel got closer and closer until we could see that the ship that was narrowly missing us was a cruise ship. We ran parallel to the ship for no more than 30 seconds before it disappeared into the stormy night. We were within a few seconds of almost colliding with a boat that was maybe 500 feet long. We were close enough that I could hear the band playing on the ship. We bobbed up and down in the ship's wake like we were rubber duckies in a bathtub. It was one of the closest calls with death that any of us would ever have. The "near miss" had terrified us. Later on I asked Captain John what words he was saying as he steered the boat south to miss the cruise ship. He said they were just a few words he learned to say back in Pilot's School. Yeah, right!

Our time in Nassau was wonderful but our main theme of conversation was about why God chose to save us that eventful night in the storm. We sailed for home early Saturday morning and with a tailwind we arrived back in Miami in the middle of the afternoon. Some of the youth were going to tell the story of the "almost tragedy" to their parents. Others were going to be mum about it since that might cause their parents to keep them from taking adventurous trips again. As for Captain John and I, we believed we were safe to go again. We believed Jesus is still patrolling the stormy seas.

Little River Springs

When I was in my first pastorate in Jacksonville, Florida, I decided to change the scope of the camp and conference program which up to that time had been limited to a small location near a 10 acre lake an hour south of the city. My idea was to take a canoe trip down the Suwannee River.

My inspiration for the canoe trip was meeting Robert Allen in 1972, a student at Columbia Theological Seminary in Atlanta, from which I graduated five years earlier. Robert was the son of the founder of the Silver Springs Reptile Institute in Ocala, Florida, where he had learned to expertly to handle poisonous snakes. Robert knew how to retrieve snake venom to make anti-venom for people who had been bitten by rattlers or moccasins. So when he volunteered to help me learn about the Suwannee River I wisely took him up on his offer. He wanted me to know what I was facing. He also wanted to teach me a little about venomous snakes. I agreed so long as I didn't have to handle them the way he could.

We picked a date, strapped a canoe over the top of his car and drove to the top of the Suwannee where the Okefenokee Swamp empties into the river. The water was brown. I couldn't see more than two feet down. At that starting point of the river it was only 25 feet wide. Later down river it would become 250 feet wide and would flow all the way to the Gulf of Mexico. We lifted the canoe off the car, placed it at the river's edge, and loaded our gear on board. A friend of Robert's drove with us, dropped us off with the canoe, and took the car three days down river to a designated pick-up place. Robert and I shoved our canoe off the sand into the cool, murky water.

As we snaked through the tight S-curves, I quickly learned several lessons. First I learned that I over-packed. The second lesson I learned was to carry thick garbage bags to put my gear in to keep the afternoon rains from soaking everything I brought. The third lesson was to exercise my shoulders and arms regularly for the week before a canoe trip because it takes muscle to paddle 20 to 25 miles a day. But most of all I learned to respect Robert and his vast knowledge of nature. He was a true outdoorsman.

Our trip went perfectly without a hitch. However, on one occasion when we had camped on the riverbank, Robert saw a rattler. He maneuvered the snake with a stick in his hand and carefully picked the snake up and placed it in a Burlap sack to carry back to the Reptile Institute. We spent 2 nights and 3 days on the Suwannee. I learned enough about the river and camping to give me confidence to lead a trip on my own. Robert went back to Ocala. I returned to Jacksonville to get 12 canoes for the first of my 18 Canoe Camps for Senior High students in Florida. In total I took approximately 700 students down the Suwannee. Thank God I brought them all home again.

The 12th year was the most memorable due to a near tragedy. It was 1983. My church kids and I were on the 6th and last day of our trip. Everyone had enjoyed the river, camping at the river's edge and growing in the fellowship that made us feel like brothers and sisters. Best of all we had played in the beautiful springs that line the river on the 90-mile trip. Some of the springs were small, not more than 30 feet wide and 6 feet deep. Others were 150 feet wide and 90 feet deep. We swam in the clear springs, swung on the ropes that hung from trees, and best of all we climbed trees at the edge of the springs and jumped into the 72 degrees water from high above. Some of the springs offered us more natural fun than an amusement park ever could.

On that last day of camp I pulled our kids out of a lovely spring a little faster than usual. Something told me that it was time to go. I followed my intuition and got my kids canoeing on the river before they were ready. It was only the middle of the afternoon and I knew we would arrive at our last spring, Little River Springs, an hour earlier than A.T. Brown would arrive with the vans and trailers for our pickup. But I just felt it was the right move. The kids grumbled and so did I, but I followed my hunch.

About an hour later my 25 canoe campers paddled into one of the most beautiful, clear springs of all, 150 feet wide and so deep with dangerous caverns that it was a favorite hole for experienced divers. But none of us saw beauty that day. All we saw was a man and a woman standing in the water's edge screaming for us to help their friend. They told us that their friend was scuba diving with 35 minutes of air and that it had been 35 minutes since he had disappeared around the corner of a deep cavern. I feared the worse.

As the rest of the canoes arrived at the spring, two of my campers who were both Eagle Scouts with swimming merit badges heard the bad news. Without apparent fear for their lives the boys dove into the spring, swam against the current of the swift hole, and disappeared around the corner into the darkness. I suggested that we pray for the swimmers. We did some of the strongest praying that any of us had ever done. My son, Mark, also dove into the spring to help. I could still see his feet at the mouth of the cave about 12 feet down when the three boys came dragging in tow a man who was limp from head to toe.

At the spring's shore they quickly pulled off the diver's tank and mask, then removed his flippers. Then the two scouts took turns giving artificial respiration to the man. His lips were blue. He was lifeless. He looked dead to me. We continued to pray, asking God to save the stranger. It seemed like an hour, but I think it was more like three minutes when out of his mouth flowed enough water to give him a chance at life. The scouts continued their work without giving up on the diver. My campers continued to pray our prayers out loud. I didn't know that I had so many committed Christians on the trip until that moment. Suddenly the diver gasped, expressed more water, and moaned like a sea lion. We softly thanked God. We cheered quietly. The diver sat up and we cheered loudly. The diver didn't smile for at least twenty minutes but we did his smiling for him. And his friends were ecstatic, yet prayerful themselves, down on their knees by their friend, who was dead but now alive.

After a half hour or so our stranger became somebody with a name and a history. Now he had an amazing story to tell about God's intervention. We shared our faith with the three men. I don't suppose they'll ever forget us. We'll never forget them either. And the two Eagle Scouts, well, there will be a special crown for them when they go through heaven's doors. Since that day I've been especially attentive to my intuition. It hasn't failed me yet. God hasn't failed me yet either, and never will.

Drifting Toward Catastrophe

After a successful sailboat voyage to the Bahamas with sixteen high school kids in the summer of 1971, I decided to offer the same experience in July of 1972. Presbyterian kids from around the state of Florida gathered at the port in Miami, walked on board the sailboat "Safe Passage," a 57 foot Ketch, and were greeted by me and Captain John, a tall and lanky fellow in his early thirties. Captain John walked us about the sailboat from stern to bow, explaining how to hoist and trim the sails. We learned that only a few of the kids had ever been on a sailboat and none of them had made a deep-water crossing in the ocean. Walking through our sleeping quarters and galley area below the deck was stuffy due to the Miami sun.

Since we had made it clear on the application that everyone had to be a swimmer to qualify for the trip, we asked the girls to bring their duffle bags on board, go below, and return with their swim suits on for their swimming tests. I jumped off the boat first with a life vest on just to make sure if one of the kids didn't swim well and needed help that I'd be there quickly to help them. The girls jumped into the beautiful blue-green water one by one and swam the length of the boat and back. They all passed the test. The boys followed the same instructions from me and all of them passed the test also. Most of the kids could swim well, except for one boy who was tall and skinny and slapped at the water instead of pulling with a smooth stroke. I told his parents that he would have to wear a life vest at all times and they agreed.

Captain John started the diesel and began steering us from the dock on a Saturday around 10 AM. The entire crew of 18, including Captain John and me, waved goodbye to parents who looked both happy to have the kids out of the house for a week but also a bit anxious to let them go on such an adventuresome voyage. I yelled a last minute message," I'll bring them home safely." Within thirty minutes we were out of the Miami harbor and on our way to Bimini for three nights. But instead of being picked up by a friendly wind we had to motor for more than hour before we could cut the motor. Our sails filled and our spirits soared. Our boat was doing what it was designed to do.

When the wind died again around 2 PM Captain John suggested that the kids jump into the ocean with their life vests on. So half the crew and I enjoyed a ten minute swim next to the boat. Captain John said we were safe there and that we didn't have to worry about sharks. Since he was a veteran of the seas we believed in his judgment. In hindsight I would have disclosed my second thoughts about our safety. But we enjoyed the swim and climbed on board for the afternoon trip into the Bimini Harbor, scheduled for approximately 6 PM.

I think the kids and I had our best times in Bimini. The small island offered one road down the middle of the island. There were no cars. The transportation was either by motorbike or by foot. Many of the kids rented bikes and rode up and down the small island from end to end. There were many small restaurants lining the streets that were not beautiful to behold but they served delicious, fresh seafood brought in daily from the charter boats. We only ate in a restaurant on the island once during our three nights on the island. Our budgets were thin. We prepared the rest of our meals on our boat. Some of them came from a can but we also ate fresh grouper that we caught from the "Safe Passage."

The island gave us time to get acquainted and offered us a place to explore our needs, our faith, and our questions about life. We enjoyed Bible discussion groups on the deck of "Safe Passage" which caused neighboring boat passengers to ask what we were doing. It was a real privilege to observe the kids relating to the fishermen. Their faith was more mature than I anticipated.

The water was crystal clear so we swam around the sailboat and snorkeled to see what the Caribbean offered below. It was thrilling to enjoy the colorful, fascinating fish below us. But it was the fishing boats that brought us the most excitement. Every morning six or eight charter fishing boats would leave to fish for grouper, sea bass or most anything that would bite. Other boats were rigged to catch sharks. In the late afternoon the boats would dock near ours and the sights were astonishing. Some of the delicious eating fish like grouper weighed at least one hundred pounds. The sharks were the big catch. None of us had ever seen a seven foot Tiger shark before. Some of them weighed three hundred pounds or more. The fishermen let us rub their catch. We were surprised to learn that sharks were smooth and not scaly. Bimini was an exhilarating place, almost an out-of- time zone for us.

Honeymoon Island was the next stop. I didn't tell the kids where we were going for the next night and day. I wanted to surprise them. So Captain John sailed us south for a couple of hours past several islands. Just before noon we anchored in about 20 feet of water, approximately 100 yards off a deserted island. It was called Honeymoon Island. It was no larger than a city block. I announced that this would be our home for the next 24 hours. From the boat we could see typical, thick tropical growth 8 to 10 feet high. Most beautiful of all we could see a pristine, white sand beach that looked like no humans had ever walked on it.

Most of the crew swam ashore. I required that they wear their life vests just in case somebody got fatigued. The distance was not more than a hundred yards from the boat. A few kids made lunch for the beachcombers and brought it to us on the beach in the dingy. Captain John stayed on board along with a few kids who were apprehensive about the swim." The day was fabulous. We swam, sunbathed, ate lunch and created games to play in the sand with large and small conch shells. Our sandcastles produced blue ribbon quality in any venue.

When it was turning dark and time to eat supper we swam back to the boat. In a way it was good to be back on board. Pristine living had its limits. After supper, stories and discussions, most of the kids fell asleep, some below and some on deck. Those of us who slept on deck watched a star shower that exceeded our imaginations. Most of us fell asleep before midnight. Captain John went below to his quarters with the instructions to call him if we saw anything unusual. I couldn't imagine what that could be and fell asleep around midnight. It was the quietest sleep I had ever known. Except for the relaxation of small waves breaking on shore it was quiet. No airplanes, trucks, sirens, nothing just quiet.

But in my sleep I began to hear louder rush of the waves. I checked my watch. It was four A.M. I opened my eyes to learn that our sailboat's anchor had slipped, and we were dragging dangerously close to the waves on the beach. We were close to beaching our boat without a way to leave Honeymoon Island. I screamed as loud as I could to alert Captain John. When he came on deck he quickly transformed his vocabulary from a Saint's to a Sinner's. The words he spoke in our emergency were not fit for Sunday School, that's for sure. If he cranked the engine and it struck the sand he would be unable to move the boat. He had no choice. He cranked the engine. It sounded loud and rough. We were in the sand. Captain John held the throttle at low speed and little by little we came out of the beach sand and made it far enough out to sea to anchor in deeper water again. A close call! Another half hour and we would have been wedged between the sand and corral that was under us. We would have had to put out an S.O.S. and abandon ship.

On Wednesday we headed north for Nassau. On the way we were going to pass Great Isaac's Lighthouse, the oldest and highest lighthouse in the Caribbean. It could be seen from 23 miles. As we passed it we saw a man standing and waving a white towel in our direction. Captain John motored us close enough to see that the man was in distress. Two kids and I went ashore and learned that the lighthouse keeper had a painful abscessed tooth. His every-two-week supply boat was not due for another week and he had no aspirin. I returned to the boat, got a bottle of aspirin, and returned to give it to him. A dentist would visit the lighthouse later in the week to pull his tooth.

A few hours later we arrived in Nassau for a two-night stay. Since it was a commercialized town with many tourists, I gave strict rules for their time away from the boat. They had buddy checks, prohibition on alcohol, and an 11 o'clock curfew. I warned the 18 year olds to steer clear of all the gambling casinos. As far as I know they obeyed my rules. But on the second night of our Nassau visit I was on the boat when a man with a Caribbean accent approached the boat with two of my kids and said that I was under arrest for contributing to the delinquencyof minors by letting them drink alcohol. He almost had me convinced that I was headed for jail. When I asked him for his badge and he said he had left it at home, I knew he was setting me up for a big joke. The kids loved watching me sweat it out.

On Saturday we set sail for Miami. The trip back seemed sad for most of the kids. Their enjoyment of each other had grown. Deep friendships had developed. Many of them planned ways and times when they could get together again. Since the kids lived in towns all the way from Pensacola to Miami it would take real commitment to travel those miles. Our docking in Miami was quiet. I felt like a Dad who had been watching over his 16 children. I was glad I brought them home again.

Creative Expressions

Out of Body

My good friend, Angus Theopolis Brown, who was known as A.T., was our wonderful Presbyterian Camp and Conference Director in the Tampa Bay area for many years. He and his wife, Doris, were truly Mr. and Mrs. Hospitality for thousands of people who came to Cedarkirk every year. A.T. and Doris are two of the most loved people I know. They've retired now to Black Mountain, N.C. A life-changing event in A.T.'s childhood prepared me for a similar event years later.

A.T. and his two ten year old friends often played in a sand pit in Laurenburg, N.C. One day they decided to dig a cave out of the side of the sand wall. They worked hard and before long they were able to crawl into the dark hole and rest from their labor. Suddenly the carved out cave fell in on them. His friends were on the edge of the cave and crawled out to safety. A.T. was at the back of the cave so he was trapped inside. He found himself in dead silence. He couldn't call to his buddies because at least two tons of sand surrounded his face, his mouth and his lips. He tried to move but the weight of the sand molded itself around A.T.'s body. He was totally immobilized and he realized the serious danger he was in. He could no longer breathe. He wondered if this was going to be his burial ground, and if so, would his soul go to heaven or not.

A.T. hoped his friends got out in time before the cave trapped them but he had no way of knowing if they escaped. If his buddies made it out A.T. knew that he would be rescued soon. A.T. thought momentarily about his family and wondered if he would ever see them again. Without knowing just how long it had been since the cave covered him, something happened to him that is hard to believe. He began hearing the most beautiful music he had ever heard. There were strings and horns and the sounds of a lovely orchestra. Then A.T. saw the doors of heaven opening for him to enter. He had no fear at all. He felt at complete peace. Time was timeless. He envisioned himself free in spite of the fact that he was imprisoned in sand. Everything was totally good. He was free from all earthly concerns.

After failing to dig A.T. out of the sand, his friends ran for help. One ran for A.T.'s Dad. The other ran to the nearest house where Mr. Garfield, the janitor at the Methodist Church, lived. Mr. Garfield ran quickly to the sight of the sunken cave, dug A.T. out, and drove him to the hospital where he regained consciousness two hours later. Recently A.T. said that his burial in the cave changed his life. He no longer took life for granted. It made him want to live a life of service for others. Since his rescuer, Mr. Garfield, was a black man, A.T. has enjoyed long time friendships with African-Americans. A.T. is now in his eighties, yet he vividly remembers the details surrounding his astounding story.

A.T. shared this story with our Covenant Group, a group of 7 ministers, in 1974. He had always been reluctant to tell this story to anyone because he was afraid someone might consider him strange. He also didn't want anyone to think he had made up the story, But in the security of our Covenant Group he gave us the privilege of believing in its authenticity. We had heard about stories like his but until we heard his story, we had wondered if there was some ulterior motive behind all of them. Not anymore. A.T. convinced us that there is a real place called heaven.

Boosted by A.T.'s courage, I told my story to the group. I felt vulnerable even though I was among the best friends of my life.

When my family moved from Jacksonville to Clearwater, Florida, in September of 1972, we helped carry the furniture in the house, received enough food and desserts to last us six months. I went outside to mow the back lawn before we would let our 4-year-old son and our 2-year-old daughter play there. So I rolled the mower to the back, took off my t-shirt, cranked the mower and began the task. It was fairly easy to do, except for having to dip under the low lying limbs of the loquat tree that scraped along my back. The long stemmed branches from a bush near the back fence were not a problem but I did have to brush through them to cut the grass close and neat.

As I walked through the branches I noticed some leaves on my stomach and knocked them off with the back of my hand. They stung but I didn't think much of it until it happened again. This time I realized that I had more stings but I could see that I didn't have leaves on my chest but saddleback caterpillars. I had been stung at least four times, maybe more, from very poisonous caterpillars. It didn't cross my mind that I was highly allergic to the stings of most anything: honeybees, wasps and bumblebees and that I had experienced troubling reactions to them in the past. Sometime later I found myself lying on my back on the cold terrazzo floor in our kitchen, having a difficult time breathing. The ceiling was going around and around. Anne quickly called our new pediatrician who told Anne to hang up and call the hospital. Anne briefly described my situation to the doctor in the emergency room and he urged Anne to get me in the car and bring me to the hospital immediately.

I don't remember getting into the car with Anne, Mark, and Julie. Neither do I remember being helped out of the car into a wheel chair at the emergency room entrance at Community Hospital. The first thing I can remember is hearing the doctor call out Code Blue! Code Blue! I became aware of numerous medical personnel entering the area where I was laid out on a stretcher. Time went by, I don't know how long. I remember only the awareness that I must be in serious trouble to have so many people scurrying all about me. That's when I went out like a light. The next interval of time couldn't be measured with this world's clocks. But what a time I had! I found myself looking down on myself on the stretcher. I could see the doctors and nurses from high above them. I felt such a peace and wanted the medical team not to worry about me because I was feeling very much at home with myself. It was unlike any worldly peace that I had ever known.

Beautiful music was playing and I saw the door to heaven open to me. It offered the brightest light I'd ever seen, but the light was not glaring. It was filled with colors like a rainbow. I felt like I needed to make a decision to enter heaven or to stay on earth. That decision, however, was not stressful. I felt like I was dancing with God and Anne at the same time. Both choices were supreme. I remember the freedom of time and place. There was no hurry. There was only the joy of the moment. The peace I felt during those hours elevated my awareness of the amazing beauty of heaven. I wanted to be there, to enter into the place that Jesus prepared for me. As I looked down on the table where the medical team was working to save my life, I wanted to be able to communicate to them that I was all right and not to work so hard. I was ready for life everlasting.

Two hours from the time I entered the emergency room at the hospital the doctors brought me back from unconsciousness. One of them came out and told Anne that they almost lost me, that I almost died on the table from shock. It took me a few days to get over it. God had given me more time on earth for love and service. However, I remembered then and still remember today the power of my "in between" experience, my out of body experience, as some people say.

It's okay for some critics to simplify what happened to me as the result of shock or perhaps medications that were given to me during the two-hour time period when I was unconscious. That would be a medical explanation. But no hallucinatory drugs were given to me that would have caused it to occur. For me it was a spiritual experience where God offered me the opportunity to see the joy of heaven. I've not regretted living on earth because I've had a marvelously full life filled with amazing grace from God. But when I'm called to go Home I'll be more than ready.

The Raccoon Sings

I loved playing guitar when I was teenager. My church youth group thought I was the Elvis Presley of spiritual singing when I would lead them in songs like "Sweet Low, Sweet Chariot" and "This Little Light Of Mine." But time passed and I put my guitar in my closet. Through my college, seminary, and the days of my first pastorate, I seldom thought about playing. It took a period of deep depression to inspire me again to begin humming tunes, to quietly sing lyrics to songs I'd never heard, and to occasionally play my old, inexpensive guitar when I was alone.

It was 1972. Anne and I had just moved from Jacksonville, Florida to Clearwater, Florida. Our marriage was on the brink of drowning in Tampa Bay and I wondered if we should seriously consider divorce. I was at the lowest point of my life. Somewhere from the depths of my soul, I began to hear music playing. So I saved the money to buy a new guitar, which I bought for $350, a pricey instrument at the time. It was a sweet sounding Gibson, so sweet that I could play chord after chord for long periods of time.

It relaxed me during a highly stressful time and escorted me into a new and productive future. My original tunes were all blues in the beginning but over the next few months I began writing humorous ballads and songs with catchy tunes that were singable for young and old. My Gibson and song writing took my mind off the troubling days of my marriage and on to a gift from God that sustained me emotionally until the sunshine could warm up my emotional life.

In early 1973 I met a man, Tom Schneider, a 21-year-old guitarist from Fort Wayne, Indiana, who got fed up with college at Ball State and had come South for the winter. We met each other at Mose Henry's home.

Mose was a mutual friend of ours who had built a recording studio and was looking for new talent. Since he had sung with The Highwaymen, a group much like the Kingston Trio, we knew he might be helpful in our singing and song writing. His studio was a makeshift, sound proofed room in his garage that had no air conditioning. Mose suggested that Tom and I record a few songs together. From the very beginning Tom had a sense that something good was happening. We played and sang together for the next 12 years at more than 300 concerts. We sang at five weeklong events in North Carolina, Alabama and Florida. One summer we toured for four weeks from Florida to West Virginia with my family also.

Our work together and our relationship as brothers of the faith were always loving and constructive. I never got tired of writing songs or playing gigs with Tom. I wrote most of the songs that we sang and Tom arranged them. I played rhythm and sang the melody. Tom played lead and sang harmony.

One of the most enjoyable songs that we wrote together was the "Raccoon Song." It was inspired one evening while Tom and I were practicing in my church office. A raccoon came to our door, stood on his back feet and looked through the window at us. Maybe he wanted a handout; perhaps he liked our singing. Who knows? But immediately Tom and I began joking about the Biblical meaning of the raccoon's visit and quickly the song began to take shape.

Over the years the song surfaced as one of the favorites of our audiences. While the lyrics affirm the goal of every church to be welcoming to every person who enters its doors, the song also uses the life of a raccoon to symbolize that hope for the world. I still can't sing the "Raccoon Song" without smiling.

Raccoon Song

Last night I was pickin' and singin' some songs
In the church with my best friend,
We were singin' them loud, we were singin' them long
We were having some fun and then,
I heard a little bump that made me sorta' jump,
It sounded like a noise outside,
I opened the door and across the floor walked a raccoon
And he cried.............(chorus)

    Chorus

I could use some fellowship, I could use a friend,
I could use a hug or two, my mask is getting' thin.
I'm tired of going to masquerades, I'm tired of playing those games,
You know who I really am, you even know my name,
I'm a Coon, a lonely raccoon.

So Tom and I listened to the Coon a while, and what a sad tale he told,
It seems he'd tried to be himself but his friends left him out in the cold,
Every move he made, he dug a deeper grave,
and he said "I'd rather be dead,
So I did what I could and Tom hugged him good,
And this is what the raccoon said..............(chorus)

So I gave him some bread and Tom gave him some wine
And we gave him all the love we had,
We spread the Good News that God cares about coons,
And the Good News made him glad,
He said, "I'm glad I'm a coon and I'll be back soon,
But I gotta' tell the world today, that the Good Lord gives
Every coon that lives the hope and the power to say".........(chorus)

Tom Schneider, the Music Man

I arrived at a friend's hot garage one June afternoon in Clearwater, Florida. Mose Henry had invited me and a few others to try out the new recording studio that he had built. Mose put me on a stool in the booth, asked another fellow to get in with me and for us to play a song for a sound check. I introduced myself. The other fellow said his name was Tom Schneider. I began to sing into the mike one of the songs I had recently written. Tom, who knew nothing about me and had no experience with my songs, began to play lead and sing harmony right away. It was amazing to me that he was so musical. We sweated through a few songs and decided we'd had enough when our sweaty fingers kept slipping off the frets. Agreeing that our time together was fun, we decided that a second practice session just might produce something we could share with a group such as at a coffee house. Tom's caring style and ability to compromise on arrangements of a few songs resulted in a good sound, so we began meeting twice a week and arranged a few more.

In August I was invited to speak in October to a weekend youth conference near Jacksonville. I agreed on the condition that Tom and I sing the message with our newly composed Christian songs. We led worship 5 times and our music was a big hit. Kids were singing and cheering. That event changed our lives. Over the next ten years we sang nearly 300 "gigs" in Florida and across the Southeast. We considered a full time music ministry but discerned that I needed to spend more time with my family. Tom and I trusted God and each other, encouraged each other when we needed help, and loved each other in the way soul brothers do. Tom married Jane Gray and they moved to Boston to work on a Masters in music. That was the end of a great period in our lives but our memories and paths still occasionally cross, though not frequently enough. Tom's song, "Willow Tree," says a lot about his character:

You are the willow, And I am the storm.
And you will bend when my winds blow
But if your roots run deep
And if your trunk is strong
You will never go down.

The Drawbridge Dragon

When Tom Schneider and I traveled south from Clearwater, Florida to Bradenton, Florida to work in a recording studio we always passed over a drawbridge that connected St. Petersburg to Bradenton. One afternoon when we had finished recording a few of our songs in Mose Henry's makeshift studio, which was housed in his garage, we headed home for Clearwater and some home cooking.

It was a lovely day that reminded us of the beauty that God provides us in the skies and the seas. We talked about the truth that we often can't see clearly what God is up to, but the afternoon sunset seemed more than enough to prove His presence. The 5 PM traffic was heavy. As we approached the drawbridge we had plenty of time to cross over it safely. The bridge tender was keeping several boats motoring in a circle.

Suddenly without warning us the bridge opened its mouth like a steel dragon, ready to swallow us whole, car and all. Wondering how the bridge was raising without adequate warning I quickly braked as hard as my foot would jam against the floorboard. The iron crossbar dropped like a giant sword onto the hood of my car. It bounced once and jumped over my Datsun like a track star jumping over a hurdle. That may have saved our lives.

We skidded out of control. I could see the drawbridge widening its mouth. Just when I thought we were avoiding disaster, I looked into my rear view mirror and saw a car bearing down on us at perhaps 50 MPH. The driver of the Ford, like me, had not seen the crossbar come down. My prayer was as quick as a falling star. I could in an instant see the faces of my family flying past my eyes. The Ford crashed into the rear of our car, pushing us up the drawbridge ramp. In order to avoid going straight over the end of the bridge and into the bay, I turned my car to the right toward the guardrail on the side of the bridge. The impact of the rear end collision sent our car crashing into the rail so hard that the car stood up vertically on its front end. We were stranded, looking straight down into the water, wondering if this was the time to say goodbye before we went head first into the bay. Another foot upward and we definitely would have somersaulted into the water. It seemed like we were stranded in our near death position for an hour but as fast as we went up, we came back down on the bridge with a crash like a heavy weight boxer from a knockout punch.

Our heads rang from the collision. We were in shock, almost senseless, even numb to the life threatening crash. For a minute Tom and I just stared at each other. Slowly our heads began to clear and we asked how the other felt. Both of us reported we had loud ringing in our ears that prevented us from hearing well, but we thought with no serious injury, though my lower back was hurting. (That back injury would follow me through all my life.)

We thought about the people in the car behind us. We climbed out of the driver's side window since the door was smashed shut and the window glass knocked out. My car looked like a green accordion. Tom's passenger side door was also jammed. The people in the Ford were unhurt since their car was larger than ours. Standing outside the car Tom suddenly grew alarmed. His guitar was in my trunk that took the brunt of the collision. The owner of the car that had rear-ended us got a crowbar out of his trunk and pried open mine. Tom's guitar was in splinters. The fret-board was broken from the body of the guitar and the strings were hanging loose. Tom pulled out his guitar and held it like it was his dead baby.

My guitar had been in the back seat. I pulled it through the back seat window since the back the back doors had been jammed by the collision. When I opened the case it looked okay. (My insurance ended up covering the purchase of a new guitar for Tom, so all was not lost.)

When the Highway Patrolman arrived we were not in good shape but we did our best to describe the way the accident occurred. The driver of the Ford did too. We claimed that the bridge tender was at fault for lowering the crossbar without warning lights. Our request was that the patrolman pay a visit on the bridge tender to discover if he was drunk or perhaps too sleepy to manage his job. We never found out the result of that visit. Maybe in the shock of our accident we didn't press our case hard enough.

Tom and I recovered from the accident, you might say. However, my back has been a constant problem for me since that day in 1974. I've had three surgeries to repair parts of my back since then and have to be careful to manage my pain daily.

I believe that God saved us from death that afternoon high upon the drawbridge. All of us have at least one key event in our history that sets apart one period from the next. Escaping from the mouth of the steel dragon is one of mine. It helped me focus on the truth that music would be the soul of my life for the next eleven years.

Music In St. Croix

During a wonderful period of our lives from 1972 to 1983 Tom Sch-neider and I played our guitars and sang in more than 300 churches and conference centers. Most of them were for Presbyterians but we occasionally had a gig for Episcopalians or Methodists. We even did a gig for a state political pep rally. We sang for groups as small as 25 and as large as 1500. During this time period I was also the minister of the Hope Presbyterian Church in Clearwater, Florida, where my church officers generously gave me the freedom to be away one day a week so that Tom and I could follow God's leading in our music ministry with people throughout the Southeast.

By far the most exotic invitation came in 1976 from a church in St, Croix in the Virgin Islands. An elder in a Dutch Reformed congrega-tion heard us lead worship in Montreat, North Carolina, and believed that Tom and I were just the ones to lead her people in a weekend renewal of their faith. We planned our trip, developed our worship plans, and gladly included Anne just for fun. I couldn't have her miss such a great opportunity to travel out of the country for the first time.

Since we were traveling with our guitars and would have to put them in the checked baggage we knew of the risk of damage. We did loos-en all of our strings in hopes that they wouldn't pop. We took along extra strings and a box of our songbooks with our original songs for the congregation to sing by. The take off from Tampa was smooth and our conversation was lively. This was going to be our best weekend yet. Landing at Saint Croix on an airstrip not much longer than the size of a football field required specially equipped engines with pow-erful back thrusts. The roaring sound made my heart pound as the air-craft rattled to a stop with only 50 yards from the end of the runway. It made me wonder about our return flight. How could an aircraft gain enough speed to lift off and clear the mountains that surrounded the airport?

The only thing on our minds as we disembarked was the state of our acoustic guitars. Without them we would be hard pressed to find other instruments that could replace our expensive ones that provided the sound we needed. We waited anxiously for the baggage to come down the ramp. The instruments appeared and seemed to be in one piece. But the true revelation of the guitars shape would be known when we opened the cases. We snapped open the locks with a strong prayer that the wooden bodies of the guitars would not be in splinters. They were both okay. Tom and I deeply breathed a sigh of relief.

The elder, Francis Krunston, loaded us, our guitars and our songbooks into a small van and we made our way around hairpin curves that occasionally overlooked the ocean. Arriving at her home was a shock because it was so tiny. Anne and I shared a small bedroom. Tom slept on the couch. The bathroom spoke to the water shortage in Saint Croix. A sign over the commode read, "In the land of sun and fun, we never flush for number one." It was a reminder that in the U.S. we have endless resources of water, gasoline, electricity, and food.

Then it was off to see the church. I felt excited from the moment I saw it. It was an old church, built in 1810, made of wood with steps of stone. It seated approximately 200, about the size of my Hope Church in Clearwater that was built in 1968, 158 years later. The pews were in the round, giving the sanctuary a warm feeling. The floors were wooden, a low cut pulpit reached out to the first pews no more than 8 feet away, and a cross hung from the wall just behind the pulpit. There were no stained glass windows but they were unneeded. There was no glass in the windows. The wooden shutters opened to the natural light.

On the right side of the church the windows opened to the placid scene of a steep downhill lined with shops until they reached the beautiful bay waters. On the left side of church the windows opened to a lovely garden with flowers blooming and birds singing. It was almost like a movie. Since it was 5 PM Tom and I set up the sound equipment and talked about the song set that we would sing for our Saturday Night performance. We unpacked and tuned our "Gibsons" and rehearsed for 45 minutes until it was time to enjoy a meal and fellowship with the congregation.

By 6:30 PM the people began heading for the sanctuary for our 7 PM concert. We hustled through our meal and followed them. The lights were on but they were hardly needed since the daylight still made the church bright. We tuned up again and softly played a few chords to warm our fingers up for the first song. We were introduced by our elder friend in such a way that is usually reserved for the famous. But we simply smiled and enjoyed every minute of it. Besides, Tom and I had been singing together for four years and we had developed a very smooth, contemporary Christian music sound. We also were one of only a few groups doing Contemporary Christian music in the U.S.

After an enthusiastic applause we took our places, I on a stool, Tom standing to my right. My music stand was in front of me where my Songbook with all the lyrics was placed. We sang a few songs, "Take-stock Of Your Life," "Praising The Lord's So Easy," and "Be The People Of God," then a wind blew my songbook across the floor during our singing of "Lilies Of The Field." Since "Lilies" had five verses to it I had to shorten the song by cutting the last two verses. I just couldn't remember them. When Anne retrieved the songbook I was relieved and I then attached a large clip to hold the book on the music stand. The evening was a big hit. The surprisingly loud applause almost seemed unnecessary but we read it to be a great appreciation of our coming so far to be with them. I'm also sure that our music was spiritually satisfying.

Our concert ended about 9 PM but the congregation hung around until 10 PM just to ask us questions about our lives and our style of music. They wanted most of all to hear us talk about our faith and motivations for our way of life as musicians. I think that the best hour of our time in St. Croix was the time right after our Saturday night concert. It provided us with a give and take with the congregation that filled our souls to the brim. Music is a medium that touches us like no other art form. Tom and I understood what was happening. Music is a spiritual magic that God surely created for our Christian growth and enjoyment.

Leading Sunday morning worship at the 11 AM hour was the climax of our Renewal Weekend. It went smoothly. Everyone sang our songs with energy. I didn't preach. Instead I gave interpretations of the songs we sang and asked the people to consider their meaning. When the worship service was over we had the feeling that we had found a second home. Everyone gathered around to thank us for our leadership and inspiration. I think we could have sung all afternoon.

However, we had other plans for the afternoon. We had been invited to go sailing on a boat owned by one of the members. We arrived at the dock, boarded a 35 foot boat, motored out of the harbor into the most beautiful, blue green, crystal clear water we had ever seen and set sail for a beach that was voted one of the top ten beaches in the world. An hour later we anchored in a bay that looked like a horseshoe with mountains on three sides and a lovely beach in the cove.

Anne and I paddled the dingy ashore. Tom swam alongside. It was unbelievably romantic with palm trees that were filled with coconuts. It had a quietness unlike any place we had ever visited.

Sunbathers were bronzed with the aid of Hawaiian Tropic, the kind without sun block, since there was not yet a medical advisory regarding skin cancer. Swimmers frolicked in the perfectly clear surf. When we decided to take a walk I surprisingly noticed that one end of the cove had nude bathers on land and sea. I waited to see how long it would take for Anne and Tom to see that we were the only ones on the south beach with bathing suits on. When I suggested that we also go nude Anne quickly ended the discussion before it was off the ground. Tom suggested that if we didn't undress that we needed to walk back to the clothed end of the island. I'll have to admit, it was exciting for a short while. After boarding our sailboat and returning to the harbor, we spent an evening with Francis and her friends before going to bed. It had been one of the best days of my life.

The next morning we boarded the plane for Clearwater and remembered how the incoming plane shook us half to death as it landed. Now we were getting on the same plane for the trip home. How could it possibly lift us over the mountaintops from a short airstrip? The pilot revved his engines for what seemed like an eternity before letting them go full throttle. Our heads pressed hard against the back of our seats and I prayed out loud something like "Here we go. Lord."

I'm positive that no one nearby could hear my audible prayers but I had confidence The Lord did. As we reached the end of the runway the aircraft suddenly reached for the sky like we were on a moon shot. Up we climbed over the coconut palms, lifting above a dedicated church family and most of all, over the mountaintops that attempted to keep us forever.

Move Over Alligator

On one momentous Thursday night my singing buddy, Tom, and I were returning home from Tallahassee through an area where there was swamp on both sides of the road. Suddenly the rain began falling in wind swept sheets as is common for Florida in both spring and summer. The last thing we wanted to do was drive into the dark, murky waters so we slowed down from about 60 mph to 30 mph to have better visibility. Old Highway 19 had ruts that filled with rain that made the road more like a shallow stream than a road. As the rain increased and our vision decreased I slowed our van even more. The windshield wipers couldn't clear the rain fast enough to help me see more than 25 feet ahead.

Suddenly, I had to slam on my brakes. I hydroplaned forward like a water skier behind a boat and stopped just barely in front of a 16-foot log. We thought about trying to drive around it but we judged it unwise since we were unsure about the safety of driving off the pavement. I could hardly believe that the log moved but something out there did. The rain quickly stopped as fast as it began. Lord only knows, the log was now a gator, the biggest I had ever seen. I hit my high beam, then back to the low, and did that a few times believing the light would scare the huge reptile off the highway but the gator didn't budge.

The road was his, he owned it, and he knew it. I thought about driving over him but I respected him and his place in the plan of nature so I tossed that option out. He blinked his eyes in my headlights, took a step but that was all. Tom and I were stuck in the swamp until the gator decided to return to his home. We sat there on the most desolate piece of highway in all of Florida wondering what to do. So I began to blow my horn, once, twice, ten times at least and the gator slowly left the highway, taking his time, just to remind us that we might have a four wheel vehicle but that he had four feet and a tail that would take him places we couldn't dream of going.

As Tom and I continued on our way home our conversation began to have a mind of its own. We stopped at the first Mom and Pop restaurant we came to, went inside and wrote the lyrics and tune to "Move Over Alligator." It has an upbeat rhythm and blues sound.

Chorus

Move over alligator, sooner or later
I'm gonna' come on through,
You can do what you want
But please do it in the swamp,
Cause I don't want to mess with you.

Well, the rain was a' drenching, lightening had me flinching
Late last Thursday night.
I was driving down the road, dodging hoppy toads
My used car was running right.
19 was the number of the road I was traveling, 55 the limit on the sign
Then right before my eyes crawled a terror in disguise.
It was a gator in the lane that was mine.

A six million dollar man could've smacked him with his hand
But I was only preacher Bob.
I couldn't see a reason for a gator hunting season
That's a redneck's weekend job.
So I stomped on my brakes with everything it takes
To bring my used car to a halt,

I rolled down the glass and gave that gator some sass
Alligator, you're the one at fault.

I got tired of playing chicken, had to find a way to quicken
The stand-off that had begun.
Then his jaw began to open and I began a 'hopin'
I could face the fact the gator had won.
I sat mad behind the wheel, is my situation real
And I began to blow my horn.
The gator hissed real big and danced a victory jig
So I sat there till early morn.

Frieda And The Priest

Frieda is one of my all-time favorite people. As the pastor of the Hope Presbyterian Church in Clearwater, Florida, I knew that my love and favoritism might slip out and make somebody else feel sort of left out, but there are some people in life who blow wind in your sails and you might as well not try to conceal it. Frieda was one of those personalities who made the worst life could throw at you somehow bearable. She also made the best life can offer you seem like heaven was closer to earth than it really is, if only for a little while. If laughter is a spiritual gift then Frieda was at the top of God's chart because when she got tickled over something I said she'd slowly crescendo into hoots like a barn owl. I loved visiting Frieda in the Catholic Home where she spent the last two years of her life. She assumed it was her job to keep all the staff on their toes and to entertain all the residents who were mostly in their high eighties and nineties. She loved to jostle with me about our different places in life.

"Good afternoon, Frieda, are you in there?"

"Preacher, where else would I be, teeing off at the Country Club?"

"I mean to say, are you presentable, you know, dressed for company?

"Funny you should ask. I haven't had a dress on in more than two years, just these drab pink nightgowns that some pig farmer stitched up in his spare time."

"Frieda, is it okay to come in now? I'm getting tired of standing out here watching the nurses waltz by with their bed pans at arms length."

"What took you so long, preacher, this is just the second time you've visited me this week. I'm 85 years old, or is it 90, and an old woman needs to hold the hand of a handsome young man as often as she can before she gives up the Ghost."

"So you're on the way out, are you? You said that last year about this time and look at you, snappy and bright. The Good Lord's not going to check you out anytime soon. Must have a mission for you here at Sisters of Mercy. Like Margaret, your roommate, God might be keeping you here just to keep her company."

"You've gotta be kidding, Bob. Margaret can't hear a thing I say and when I tell her to turn up her hearing aid it shrills so loud the orderlies start running for cover in the mop closet. Sticking my fingers in my ears might not look ladylike but it keeps me from telling the old bat to take a long walk off a short pier."

"Sounds like you're pretty rough on Margaret, don't you think?" Where is she anyway?"

"Rough on her? It's the other way around. Her children come to visit her and it sounds like an Atlanta Braves game in here. They scream something like, 'The Braves won again yesterday' and Margaret says. 'Yes, I'm brave, I know I'm brave, but did you bring me any of those chocolate covered pecans today?

"I know she enjoys those chocolate covered nuts," I said.

"She does, but I don't. She'll eat a whole box of them in one morning, then all she does for the rest of the afternoon is fart. Have you ever heard a 200-pound woman let one go? It's awful. Her bed covers lift up like a hot air balloon at sunrise. I have to pull my pillow over my nose to prevent the odor from sending me prematurely to meet

Jesus. It's not easy for me to get around these days but when she starts in I get out of bed as quick as I can and head to the sunroom for an extended stay."

"Speaking of sunrooms," I said, "why don't we amble down there and pick up a few rays before the sun sets. It's getting close to supper so there will probably be a few seats open. You need to walk as much as you can. Let's just take it slow."

"Listen preacher, anybody who wears boots to preach in, sports a beard long as Lincoln and hair as long as Jesus has no right to tell an old lady what she needs to be doing. I'm not walking for my health, only to escape for a while from my air bag roommate."

"Tell me about your nephew, Fred, how is he doing? Do you remember when he played for the Pittsburg Steelers?"

"Yes, that was back in the thirties when they got paid per game, like $25 a game and a ticket cost just $1. I never was much into being a ladylike girl but I did love my football...went to most every game... even when it was twenty degrees. Back then there would be about eight or ten thousand people at the game but we cheered like we were fifty thousand. Fred played guard. There weren't any facemasks back then but he kept playing for many years....must have broken his nose a dozen times. Ever noticed how crooked his nose is?"

"Yes, I've noticed. You do know that Fred has a serious cancer in his nose. Frieda, do you know that he will lose most of his nose in surgery next week? He'll look quite strange to us. But I know Fred can handle it. He's mentally tough. What do you think, Frieda?"

"Preacher, I think you're right. Oh, I was going to suggest that we start back to my room now but let's wait a few minutes. I just saw the new Priest go into my room and I'd like to stall here to see if I can avoid having to hear his tirade about my needing to be a Catholic on the Catholic highway to go straight to heaven. Most of the priests are warm and kind and want to know how I am before they pray for me. Father Dominic is pushy and with the personality of a porcupine. Oops, he saw me. Get ready to meet a bully."

Father Dominic walked the 30 yards from Frieda's door to the sunroom like a fullback headed for a touchdown. His clerical collar was obviously too tight because his face was three shades too pink to be human. The closer he got the more I could feel Frieda's hand become sweaty, yet firm in mine. She spoke first to the priest. "Coming to visit a devout Presbyterian, are you Dominic?

"Miss Frieda, you know good and well that my name is Father Dominic. You should offer me the courtesy of my office. I went to school and university 12 years to earn my right to this office. By the way, who is this young, wayfaring stranger, your grandson? He looks like he needs a haircut."

Frieda bristled at the slashing remark and said, "Don't get me going, Dominic, this is my preacher. He's been to school for 14 years to get his job and he wears boots for a reason."

Now Frieda," I said, "Father Dominic is here because he cares about you." I introduced myself. "I'm Bob Walkup, a Presbyterian minister. Frieda has been a member of my church for 12 years and she means a lot to all of us."

Dominic declared, "A Presbyterian is only halfway through the Holy Church. There is so much for him to do before reaching the holiness of God."

"But what about grace?" I said." Are we not saved by grace that opens the door to everyone right away? My interpretation of scripture includes the Baptists and the Catholics and everyone in between."

"That's where you're wrong young fellow, if the Vatican hasn't put the stamp of approval on your soul, then your salvation is in a constant state of flux."

"Dominic, "Frieda replied, "There are two doors into heaven. I definitely don't expect you'll be entering through the front door with me."

"C'mon Bob, let's go back to my room. Goodbye, Dominic, and you can forget about coming to visit me tomorrow. I'm always going to be a Presbyterian."

Frieda was as feisty as a mountain goat. Nothing seemed to change about her over the years that I was her minister, except her spirituality, which distributed a healthy portion of comedy to most anyone around. When I'd visit her she'd ask me to pray for her. Sometimes I would ask Frieda to pray for me, and even pray for Margaret as well. On one particular day, her words were priceless.

"Dear Lord, I'm an old woman but in my mind I still feel like a young girl. Thank you for bicycles and books of poems. Thank you for my Mom who taught me how to be a lady and for Dad who taught me how to fish. Thank you that I never married Tom because he turned out to be no good. Thank you for Fred and Dot who have taken such loving care of me for so many years. Give my minister, Bob, plenty of gas for his car so he'll visit me often. But please don't give my roommate, Margaret, any gas at all. But if you do, please help her keep it under her own sheet. In Jesus' name, Amen.

The Robe Maker and The Healer

During our ministry in Clearwater at the Hope Presbyterian Church we enjoyed the fellowship of a wide variety of interesting people. One was a Robe Maker, Mary Anne Wells, who heard of my interest in wearing contemporary worship robes. I had always worn the traditional black robe but when I attended a conference in Montreat in 1974, I saw many kinds of colorful robes being used by the worship leader. I bought several patterns for a chasuble, the kind that you drape over your head and down onto your shoulders. When I returned home I asked Anne if she would like to make one for me. She measured my height, my shoulder width, and my head size, and we chose a wine colored pattern that became my favorite robe for the first Sunday of every month when we served communion to the congregation.

But when Mary Anne Wells heard about the opportunity she quickly jumped on the task. We selected the right material for three other patterns and she was off and running with the project. One robe was going to be a coat of many colors like Joseph wore. The second was going to be a shepherd's robe with little white sheep sewn onto a coat of green to symbolize the pasture. The third was going to be white. On that robe she got the youth to stitch a cross and a rainbow. From 1974 through 1984 at Hope Presbyterian I wore these robes to help me and my flock celebrate our risen Lord. Mary Anne Wells helped set a visual aid for our worship services that allowed me to choose the robe that best fit the theme of the day. I didn't wear my traditional, black robe until I began my ministry with the Medical Benevolence Foundation.

Another key person in my life in Clearwater was Dr. Bob Wells, the husband of Mary Anne. Bob was a respected plastic surgeon in Clearwater who in 1978 began taking a serious interest in the people of Haiti, a country that was impoverished then and still is today, especially since the devastating earthquake in 2010. Back then Bob began visiting the Presbyterian Church-supported Hospital St. Croix in Leogane, a town 30 minutes from Port au Prince. He found a wide variety of needs but he decided to spend his time doing surgery on children with cleft palates, a prenatal lack of development when a split from the front to the back of the roof of the mouth fails to join together. Bob said that the problem occurred when the mother and therefore the child are malnourished during pregnancy. When Bob and I traveled to Haiti together I was privileged to scrub up and go into surgery with Bob and view his surgical skill and love for children. Bob had incredibly skilled hands. He was sure of his task and amazingly quick with his scalpel and suturing of the dear children, who over the years had been ridiculed for their abnormal facial appearance.

Bob always made his trips to the hospital for at least two weeks so that he could do surgery the first week and do follow up visits with the children the second week. One of the most inspirational times of my entire life happened as the smiling mothers of the children returned to visit Dr. Wells to show the progress their children had made in just one week. The little boys and girls would no longer be teased over their looks. They were well on their way to a normal facial appearance.

It was also Dr. Wells' commitment to better health for the children in Haiti that lit a fire under my feet for mission that has burned hot for the rest of my life. It was Dr. Wells who introduced me to Third World needs and the possibility of making a difference in so many lives. It was Bob Wells who helped our congregation invite the "Blind Boys Choir" from a Port au Prince School to visit us and provide our people with the vision of working with the Haitian people on a larger scale. After the "Blind Boys Choir" performed at Hope Presbyterian we developed a 2 cents a meal mission program that funded mission in Haiti. The plan requested that our congregation and all the congregations in Florida save 2 cents for every meal they ate and contribute the monthly amount to the fund kept at the Presbytery Office. Each quarter we would send the total amount to our Presbyterian hospital in Leogane for use with malnourished children. I had the privilege of speaking to dozens of churches about the needs in Haiti. The program spread nationwide. During the next five years, we raised $300,000 for the Haitian Feeding Program For Children. It was Bob Wells who inspired the program into reality.

Bob was so effective in getting others involved with Third World needs that in 1984 I left the pastorate for a ministry with the Medical Benevolence Foundation, an arm of the Presbyterian Church that raised funds for our Third World hospitals and missionary medical teams around the world. I served MBF for three and a half years before moving to the Saint Andrews Church in Raleigh. During my time with MBF when I was in Bangladesh, I received word that Bob Wells had taken his own life. He was buried before I retuned home. It was one of the saddest times of my life. I can feel the sadness even while I write today. Bob had gotten depressed, secluded himself from activities and stopped attending church. I had counseled with Bob about his depression previously. I had always hoped he would get the right medication and be faithful to take it. Regardless, depression kills the spirit and sometimes the body.

This letter is dedicated to one of the most influential men in my life. His vision was far greater than mine. It was Bob's love for mission that transformed mine. It was that love that linked me to Saint Andrews Presbyterian in Raleigh. More than anything else, his love for children was divine. Thank you, Bob.

Every Heart Beats the Same

Cameroon's Matthew

Cameroon was the first country I visited after being hired by the Medical Benevolence Foundation in 1984. Our son, Mark, asked if he could travel with me, even if the significant cost meant that he would have to delay going to college for a year. I agreed that it would be a worthy sacrifice for him to make, but I didn't tell him until we returned from the trip that Anne and I were going to send him to college on time anyway.

So Mark and I met Keith McCafferty, the Director of MBF, in New York and flew to Brussels on the next leg of our trip. Our next flight to Yaounde, the capital of Cameroon, was remarkable because only 20 passengers, plus 20 crew members, were on board a 747 that could hold approximately 275 people. We had the privilege of any seat we wanted. When we got tired we pulled up the armrests on four or five of the seats in the middle section and lay down for comfortable naps.

After 15 hours we landed in Yaounde. It was shocking to drive into the city to find such a bustling place. While there were many signs of poverty, there were also obvious signs that the city was prospering. I was surprised by my first view of Africa. Obviously I was going by my stereotypical view of the continent. It only took an hour to teach me that Africa is extremely diverse. I had a lot to learn, most of which can't be learned in a school classroom. I quickly learned that every heart beats the same, all over the world.

Having spent one night at a missionary's home we drove out of the city on smooth roads before slowing down due to the significant deterioration of the country roads. We had to drive our van slower and slower, no more than 10 miles an hour. There were potholes a foot deep that could cause damage to our van. My first demonstrative sign that we were in Africa was to see a dead monkey for sale, hanging on a tree limb. Someone would buy it and cook it for their meal. The only place I had seen a monkey before was in a zoo, happy and carefree, swinging from limb to limb. Not in Cameroon.

After a two-hour drive we arrived at a sleepy little town and stopped at a street-side cafe for delicious coffee, bread and butter, and some of the most delicious jam I've ever tasted. There were six or eight tables all around us, most of the diners speaking French, since Cameroon is a former French colony. The mid-morning coffee was strong and helped to perk us up from yesterday's long day of travel.

Soon we arrived at the Presbyterian Hospital. We were introduced to a small man, 5'4" tall, perhaps 140 pounds with a smile as wide as a slice of watermelon. We were told that he was one of the surgeons at the hospital. That was, however, not the primary point of amazement. We learned that Matthew had only a 6th grade education. Our missionary doctor noticed Matthew's high intelligence when he was serving as an orderly in the hospital. So the missionary doctor began teaching him all about medicine. Matthew was a quick, brilliant learner. In a brief time Matthew learned general medicine and also the skills of surgery. We were invited by Matthew to scrub up and come into surgery with him. We did and it was amazing to us. A humorous note of the story is that Matthew was so short that a special platform had to be made for him to stand on to do his work. Perhaps standing by him while he did surgery was the highlight of the entire trip for me, although many such happenings continued to come our way for the following three weeks.

Since the purpose of our trip was to observe and report our findings to our Board of Trustees we were up and out at 7 a.m. the next day to try and cover as much of the medical work in Cameroon as possible. The van was filled to the brim with Mark, Keith, and me, plus Matthew and three nurses. We packed every available space with utensils, gauze, bandages and lots of soap. Each of us held stacks of clean sheets on our laps.

A three-hour drive on awful roads brought us to at a small village where we were to do surgery. I looked about for the hospital and there was none. I was pointed toward a 20' x 50' building that was used as the community center. It was like all of the houses in the village, clay floor and thatched roof. I thought I was being humored but I soon learned that the medical team meant business. The nurses hopped out of the van and began washing down the metal tables inside the building where the surgeries were to take place. Matthew began interviewing the potential patients for surgery. When the tables were clean the nurses spread clean sheets over the tables to ensure better cleanliness. One by one, the patients were cared for by the medical team. Each patient was placed on a clean sheet on the floor after the operation was over. When I asked about post-operative complications I was told that their record exceeded the good records of U.S. hospitals. The medical team told me the success of the operations was due to the power of prayer. After three hours of surgery, we all returned to the Presbyterian Hospital. Two nurses were left behind to provide post-operative care.

On our way back to the hospital we saw more inspiring missionary action. About two hundred people of all ages were gathered around two tables under tall trees. They were all very quiet, in an almost reverent state. As we pulled our van up next to the crowd we could see that four French missionaries were trying glasses on very appreciative people. They had 7 or 8 large boxes of glasses from donors in France and one by one they matched the needs of the people with glasses from one of the boxes. It was beautiful to see the people's eyes light up and their smiles widen when the right prescription was found.

As we prepared to fly to Zaire (now Congo) the next day we knew we had witnessed many memorable events in Cameroon. God was active there.

Texas Opera In A Cold Shower

When Keith McCafferty arrived to speak at my church in Clearwater, Florida, I could tell immediately that he was a giant fellow. It wasn't his 6 foot 2 inch frame that made him big. It was the way he swaggered across the parking lot like a Texan, and mighty proud of it too. When he shook my hand I could feel a combination of power and love that actually told the story of his life. He expressed his power and love through the Medical Benevolence Foundation (MBF), which supports the medical mission work of the Presbyterian Church, USA.

That summer evening my congregation and I discovered a fellow on a mission. Keith was the Director of MBF, who raised funds for hospitals, clinics, medical personnel, medical equipment and pharmaceuticals for our denomination's mission work abroad. He developed funds to be used in lands as close as Haiti and as far away as South Korea. Keith saw neither skin color nor religion in his service around the world. Instead, Keith only saw malnourished children, kids sick with malaria, mothers with pneumonia, and men so sick they had to be carried to the hospital in a wheelbarrow. Keith's eyes were open to every possibility for servanthood. He never closed his eyes or his mind when he encountered a challenge to fill a need somewhere around the world. He was the most visionary person I've ever known. Keith raised many millions for mission from churches around the country.

In 1984 Keith invited me to join him on this team and I accepted right away. I felt God moving through him to me. Perhaps I had grown a bit bored with my pastorate, though I don't think it was the primary reason for my change of vocations. It was just his gentle and assertive manner and I always liked people who said what was on their minds. For instance, when he completed his presentation on missions, he looked at me and my officers and said, "Will you give MBF $10,000 for the hospital in Haiti?" I remember thinking that this fellow was asking for too much from my congregation. But we said, "Yes, we will!" Occasionally Keith was a bit too assertive but I would rather have a leader being too assertive than one who is not assertive enough. One of my contributions to MBF was helping Keith to tone down his energy so that he wouldn't come across to some congregations and our denominations' Mission Board like a bull in a China shop. But one thing was certain, Keith never lacked the dedication to finish a project with more enthusiasm than when he first began.

I loved to hear Keith laugh. Some folks just utter a chuckle or a muffled laughter, almost like they're embarrassed to feel the joy. But Keith would bend his back almost touching his spine with the back of his head it seemed, then with a full breath he would laugh so loudly that everyone in the room would laugh as well. And my how he loved jokes, the uplifting kind. I do have to admit that Keith took liberties with us preachers. We were always on his hit list, helping us and our congregations to see that we're just like everybody else. Since Keith saw us as we were he knew where to find our souls. Then he would lift up our Spirits and walk away with our money to support third world needs. He was really a master at that. Keith was the best advocate for missions I have ever known.

On one of our mission trips in Africa we visited Cameroon and the hospitals there. When one of our long days was over we retired early, knowing that we would need to get up the next morning at 5 A.M. to travel inland from Yaounde to work in a clinic. When we got out of bed it was quite cool, perhaps 50 degrees, and there was no heat in our guesthouse. I remember stopping the alarm clock, saying good morning to Mark, and as fast as I could, dressing warmly to fight off the chill in the air.

As Keith stepped into the shower and pulled the curtain shut I quickly informed him that there was no hot water in the house. He simply said, "What's a little ice water to a mission man?" At that he turned the water on full blast. It was his signal to sing and he belted out "O Sole Mio, O Sole Mio" from the bottom of his diaphragm as if this was the last possible chance for him to sing again. I still to this day believe that the thin metal shower stall trembled. If it didn't, I did. I had no idea Keith had such perfect pitch. He had a baritone voice that could sing solos in any choir, great or small. Little did I know that this swaggering Texan loved opera.

I guess I learned more about Keith McCafferty when I traveled with him than when I discussed mission issues over coffee back in Texas. What I learned I liked. Keith retired from MBF as a living legend. He taught me how to love people in Third World countries like he did. What a gift!

Congo Cops

It was shocking to leave a thriving Yaounde, Cameroon and fly into a disturbingly impoverished Kinshasa, the capital city of Zaire that is situated on the southwest coast of the continent. In the 90's Zaire return to its original name, Congo. Our arrival began with a long wait at the Mobutu Seke Seko International Airport. We could have moved right through but the customs officers asked us to pay $1000 to get our pharmaceuticals and operating instruments through customs. Keith McCafferty insisted that the medicine and equipment were for the health of their people and that we would not pay a bribe to get them through. Over the next two hours we sat and waited for their next best offers, which little by little decreased from a $1,000 bribe to $100. Finally we agreed to pay $50 just to get on with our visit.

One of our Presbyterian missionaries, Nancy Warlicke, who worked at TASOK, the International School for missionary children, picked us up at the airport and drove us to her family's home in the city. After a delicious meal we all talked together about our families, our schools and the ministry we enjoyed. However, the stories we heard about the city, the entire country, and about the "President for Life" Mobutu were disturbing. Mobutu's brutality and his robbing the country of its diamonds caused me to think twice before I said anything in public.

The next morning we all took cold showers because the power was unreliable. The electric stove finally started working and we enjoyed a warm breakfast. Nancy invited us to tour the safe part of the city. Our son, Mark, Nancy's son and daughter and I, crammed ourselves in Nancy's compact car and we began our rough ride by going to the Health Department which was more of a joke than a helpful resource for the community. Of the two floors of office and laboratory space only two rooms were being used. Perhaps 5 percent of the building's space had furniture. Realistically there was no work being done there. The 10 technicians seemed to have nothing to do and were sitting around, talking and laughing. It was absurd to me since the city's health conditions were terrible. Obviously the money for health concerns was being siphoned to greedy people. Since greed eats us from the inside there were certainly many people in power in Zaire who were hollow inside.

But our next visit was encouraging. We visited a missionary nurse, Annette Kriner, who was doing demanding but rewarding work in a public health clinic. In spite of the overwhelming hundreds of people who came to her clinic every month she kept her spirits up. With minimal resources of medicines, staff, and money she appeared to be providing more health care than the rest of the city altogether. I never saw another clinic the entire time we were in Kinshasa. She offered a "fight hunger" program for infants and children. I can still see the happy faces of those who ate their only meal of the day at Annette's clinic. These beautiful kids were being touched by the gifts of Presbyterians 12,000 miles away. While I had been amazed at the ministry we were doing in Cameroon I was being humbled by the sights and sounds of Kinshasa.

We paid our most memorable visit in the late afternoon. We left the Warlick's house and headed for the missionary school where Nancy Warlick was the principal of approximately 75 students whose parents were missionaries in Zaire and surrounding countries. Compared to the rest of the city school buildings the missionary school was a little bit of heaven. The teachers in the city school were paid very low salaries, if anything at all, during some weeks, but the teachers in the missionary school were paid well for their hard work. Only a small percentage of the students in Zaire schools were given the privilege of an education. The missionary school provided an excellent education for all its students. We took an hour out of our tour to play basketball at the school. It was a great release for me. I had become emotionally exhausted from seeing widespread poverty and injustice.

Eventually Nancy offered to drive us by Mobutu's Presidential Palace. She had never been there but thought it would be a memorable trip to make. We gladly hopped into the car, basketball and all, and headed across town. I had walked past the White House in Washington a few years back so I was interested in what we might see. After a 15-minute drive Nancy indicated that we were probably on the right road and to keep our eyes out for the sign. I was in the front passenger's seat so I figured that I might be the one to see a sign first. We casually passed a guard station with about a dozen soldiers with rifles in their hands.

Pow! Pow! cracked their rifles. Nancy slammed on brakes with a piercing screech that made me muffle my ears with my hands. We all froze. The soldiers quickly surrounded our vehicle screaming something with great intensity. With their rifles pointed at us they motioned us out of our car. Nancy looked afraid and I was too. I think the kids were thinking that this must be a rehearsal for a movie. We must have done something wrong but I wasn't sure what it was. We all were forced out of the car by the angry men. I remember getting sweaty fast and my heart rate increasing rapidly. I told Mark and the other kids to stand still and let Nancy do the talking. The soldiers spoke French so Nancy was the only one who could talk with them. The conversation was tense. I could see it in Nancy's eyes but she somehow was holding her ground. Her voice was strong and emphatic. The next ten minutes were the longest ten minutes of my life. I was afraid that the Warlicks and the Walkups were going to be tossed into some dark dungeon for a long, long time. As the interrogation continued I noticed that two of the soldiers were eyeing our basketball on the back seat of the car. Mark motioned that he would show it to them if they would like. A soldier moved his gun toward the ball. Mark reached in and brought the ball out. When the soldier looked puzzled Mark began dribbling it and bounced the ball to the soldier who quickly handed his rifle to his buddy so that he could catch it.

What happened next is either a miracle or is just what happens when we have a ball of any kind in our hands. We play with it. It's universal in its ability to bring out the child from within us. When we have a ball in our hands our mood turns from violent and distrusting to playful and competitive. Almost immediately we saw the face of the soldier transformed from enemy to friend. And when he passed the ball to one of the other soldiers I could feel the ice breaking. Maybe we could get out of this violation without going to prison after all. Within five minutes Mark was teaching them how to dribble and contagious laughter spread through the entire squad. The tension was broken. Nancy and the captain finished their negotiation about our potential incarceration and returned to the dribbling soldiers who were turning out to be our friends. Thank God for basketballs that are better negotiators than most astute linguists.

They ushered us back into our car. Nancy turned the car around and told us that we were lucky. The captain had first believed we were trying to go past the guard gate on purpose so that we could harm Mobutu. They were preparing to jail us and that could mean for a long time. Apparently Nancy's negotiations and the basketball joined forces to free us from Mobutu and his men. I never knew the meaning of the word "free" until that day. As we drove away we all waved goodbye and they waived back with their rifles and their smiles.

176

Mark and A Little Girl's Eyes

Flying from coastal Kinshasa in the Congo far inland to Kananga on the country's only jet plane was fairly uneventful, other than the lady in front of us climbing aboard with a scrawny hen, too skinny to lay an egg, and too bony to eat for dinner. I couldn't figure out her motive, unless it was for a superstitious ceremony for a hex or a healing. She seemed attached to the hen and held the chicken close to her breasts like many women would hold a dear child. That was okay by me until she let loose the hen who jumped on top of her seat overlooking my knees. I looked the chicken in the eye and she stared into mine so I quickly spread my knees apart in case she had passed up the ladies room back at the airport. I didn't dare doze off as I'm prone to do on airplane flights. Besides her constant clucking kept me wondering what her next move would be. Three hours later we landed in Kananga. I had clean knees. Miracles still do happen.

We were picked up at the airport by a missionary driver and carried to Tshikaji, a small village in central Congo that had the largest Presbyterian medical facility for miles around. Not only did it provide public health work but it also had an in-patient capability that drew people from many miles away. It was a good place for us to slow down and gather our feelings from our two weeks of travel. One of our fondest memories was going to a nearby small river where construction had begun on a dam. One of our missionary engineers was overseeing the project. I wish I could remember his name because he represented the dozens of missionaries around the world who were other than evangelists and medical personnel. The people in the village truly loved this good man for helping to provide electricity for them for the first time in their lives.

But the most important story is about our son, Mark, who was a rising senior at Clearwater High School in Florida. Mark was a runner on the cross-country team and needed to stay in shape. One hot afternoon Mark left the relative comfort of the Tshikaji shade to run a few miles. When the heat and the distance caught up with him he sat down outside the village to rest. He was wondering about all that he had seen and heard during the week. Thinking about the week ahead entered his mind. What was this trip all about anyway?

Then ever so lightly he felt the touch of someone behind him. Mark turned to see a little girl about seven years old with her hand on his shoulder. But he focused on the little girl's eyes, which were as beautiful as they were compassionate. He could see that she was concerned about his being so far from the village and all alone. Her love for him renewed his spirit and changed his entire concept of who he was and why he was there. The future was in the little girl's eyes. He didn't know then that he would eventually get a degree in African Studies/ Refugee Resettlement, marry a woman born and raised in Africa, a woman who spent many years of her childhood in the village where he was sitting. Mark didn't know that the very next day he would fly into an even smaller village named Bulape that was another village where his future wife, Ruth, lived during her childhood. Ruth's parents were Presbyterian missionaries. Her dad, Richard, was a medical doctor and her Mom, Judith, was a teacher.

I remember reflecting then, and again now, about the sacrifices missionaries make when they are called to go places far from their U.S. homes to serve people and nations far less affluent. Most of them could make excellent salaries back home, far more than they make on the mission field. Since the work is so difficult how can they live year after year with people who speak a language that is not their native tongue? How do they manage to live in a strange culture? I thought about their relatives and good friends back in the U.S. who must miss seeing them more often than during the month of their annual furlough.

Perhaps missionaries can hear that beat that allows them to walk to a different drummer. I don't know. I'm reluctant to say that missionaries are a special group of chosen servants. That might deny that God has chosen all the rest of us for special ministry also. Anyone who has studied the Bible knows that the Holy Spirit calls us all to service. However, after visiting missionaries in Africa I'm impressed with their ability to do so much with so little, to reach long lists of goals with a short list of supplies, to overcome obstacles that most people would judge as impossible, and to consistently listen to the spirituality that undergirds their work. One thing for sure, our trip to Cameroon and Congo has required me to listen more carefully to the beat of the Drummer in my life.

Like Coming Home

We all climbed out of bed in Tshikaji eager to take our flight to Bulape in the Congo. Our party included Mark and me, Keith Mc-Cafferty, and two new members, Larry Wood and his 16-year-old daughter, Anna. Getting to the airstrip by 9 A.M. was most important, we were told. We learned that the pilot likes to get in the air early so we ate a quick breakfast, packed our luggage for the overnight trip, and the hospital driver motored us to the side of the hangar. We hopped out and were interested that no plane was in view. A simple assumption was that the pilot hadn't returned from another missionary flight. But when we walked around the corner of the hangar we were warmly greeted by a young fellow who introduced himself as Richard Olenick. Richard was a pilot with the Missionary Aviation Fellowship. He shook our hands with his greasy ones, informing us that he was the pilot. I looked behind him and I could tell there was a small Cessna in the hangar with every piece of the motor laid out on a giant tarp. I asked him what time the plane that we were flying to Bulape was due to land. He looked at me with a big smile and said, "It's already in, this is it. In a few hours I'll have it up and running like new. Ya'll just make yourselves comfortable. There are plenty of old buckets around the hangar to sit on. I'm looking forward to flying you to Bulape."

Well, I wasn't going to be the first person to express some doubt or anxiety about the predicament that we were in. There must have been 100 parts laid out on the tarp and I had little confidence in Richard's ability to re-assemble the engine. Anybody could take one apart, even me, but not just anybody could put one back together again. Richard began to talk as he worked, reminding us that he had to overhaul the engine every 500 or so hours. When he commented that he had done this mechanical overhaul 4 times I did feel a little better, but I still had this nagging feeling that maybe Mark and I ought to stay in Tshikaji and let the other folks go ahead. But the more I watched Richard's meticulous care for each part of the engine the more I was reminded that we were on a faith journey. It took Richard about three hours but by about noon he had the plane ready to go again. I thanked God for Richard and for all my team and by the time Richard asked us to weigh our baggage I was ready to fly.

Then there was another snag in my emotions. Richard asked each of us to weigh on a scale, and then weigh our baggage. Richard indicated that we were overweight and that we either had to discard one passenger or leave a lot of our baggage behind. We began taking all non-essentials from our duffle bags, leaving us with a change of clothes and our toothbrush and toothpaste. It was a teaching moment since I remember thinking that I carry far more than is required on all the trips that I make. The only things that were non-negotiable were the medicines and medical instruments for the hospital. Richard weighed us again and told us to discard another 10 pounds. We dropped more weight in the form of shoes, a beard trimmer and a curling iron that we didn't have a power source for anyway. Richard finally was satisfied with his load, although our weight was right on the edge of safety. He pointed out the tree line at the end of the runway and laughingly told us to pick up our feet when the airplane got there.

We climbed aboard the Cessna. The adults had the four seats, of course. The teenagers, Mark and Anna, were crammed into the small storage space in the tail of the craft. Richard taxied us to the end of the strip, revved his motor for what seemed like a day, then we roared slowly, faster, much faster, but I thought we'd never lift off. As we neared the end of the dirt runway our pilot loudly said, "Pick up your feet now!" I knew then that I should have taken physics back in college so that I would know without a doubt that picking up my feet wouldn't help us get airborne anymore than a cow could jump over the moon.

So I did what Richard said to do. I picked up my feet and looked around the plane embarrassingly, hoping no one could see my feet off the floor. But I could see that I had good company. All of us had our feet in the air. I also had my hands in a prayerful position. You never know what'll help in life. Sure enough, it must have helped because the Cessna lifted off and cleared the tree line just in the nick of time. When I asked our pilot if he had ever carried this much weight before he looked into his rear view mirror, caught my eye, smiled and said, "Nope, never before." I didn't know what to say to that, so I just kept my quiet and said a few prayers, not the Sunday morning kind of prayers, more along the line of questioning my sanity.

The adults talked loudly but we could barely hear each other because of the engine noise. It drowned out most of our sentences so we relied on short phrases to communicate to each other. When I turned to see how things were going for Mark and Anna back in the luggage area, I was glad to see that they looked happy together. They really had no choice because they were packed in so tightly among the boxes and luggage that their heads almost touched. I wondered if a close relationship was developing. Looking back, Mark and Anna did grow closer as the days passed by but I think it was more of a brother and sister relationship. It could have been a romance I suppose but Mark had a girlfriend back in Clearwater. I wondered if the trip was influencing Anna's life as much as it was Mark's.

Our pilot, Richard, called out to alert everyone that we would be landing in approximately five minutes. He told us that the dirt runway was only 150 yards long, cut out of the forest like a bowl. He also told us to stay calm. Now I have to admit that when somebody tells me to stay calm that what he's actually saying is that this next situation has the potential of freaking me out. It seemed that our pilot communicated to us piece by piece. He didn't want us to know too much at one time. His next message was that due to the shortness of the runway and the high trees that encircle the runway that we would have to lower our airspeed and circle the runway two times. Richard suddenly cut his engine back. It sounded like he cut the engine off altogether, though probably not. I was holding my breath and I think a few other passengers were too. I looked into the baggage department and Mark and Anna showed no anxiety it all. They had been on rides at the County fair that were rougher than this flight.

I should have remembered Richard's experience. We were in good hands. He told us back at the hanger that he had made this flight dozens of times without incident. Apparently he could put his "puddle-jumper" down on a postage stamp. Our plane began to glide, little by little, until the angle of the plane obscured our view of the strip. I couldn't see anything but the cockpit. It felt like we had become a paper airplane, one like the children make and fly at recess. It seemed like the wind was the only thing holding us in the sky. Suddenly Richard revved his engine hard, the wings came down, the tail went up and within seconds we touched down. All of us whooped and hollered like we had won a world championship.

Hundreds of children ran out to the plane to greet us and carry our luggage for us. Amazing! Each of us felt our spirits lifted by the overwhelming appreciation that the children showed us. I still compare it to the beautiful scene when Jesus rode into Jerusalem. Of course, I know that I'm not comparing myself to Jesus but I did feel like I was a holy man when I stepped off the plane that afternoon in a remote village of Congo.

During our first three weeks in Africa I felt like a stranger but when we landed in Bulape I suddenly felt like I had come home.

Bulape Visit

When our single-engine plane made its precarious landing on a miniature dirt runway in Bulape, Congo, we all shook hands together with a combination of feelings. I almost stooped to a level of false bravado, like I had done something, when all I did was to stay seated and pray we wouldn't crash. But I also had a sense of relief with genuine thanksgiving. We had made it! No ordinary pilot could do the things Richard had to do to bring us in safely. Mark and I, Keith and Larry and his daughter, Anna, were glad to be on the ground.

Even before our plane rolled to a stop there were more children than you could count, flying with wings on their feet to greet us. They knew to stay clear of the propeller but as soon as it twirled to a halt the children gathered on all sides of the plane. The older children knew that the door to the airplane opened on the right side so they gathered there waiting for the first sign of our stepping down. The kids were cheering like we were royalty and in a way we were for them. We had come on a long journey bringing gifts. When we swung open the door their cheers were almost deafening, the way children sound when they cheer in squeals. It was unlike anything I had ever experienced in my life. Some years back I played and sang with my friend, Tom Schneider, for a large crowd of kids in Montreat, N.C. and got a standing ovation. It was loud but it didn't have the overwhelming joy of these little children. Chills ran down my spine and I'm sure to my toes as well. I had heard and read about events like this but never dreamed I'd be in the middle of one myself.

Our pilot told us that after the customary greeting and handshaking the older children would carry our luggage and boxes of instruments to our guesthouse. Keith would carry the precious pharmaceuticals himself. So we stepped down from the aircraft and gave the luggage and boxes to the older kids. Since the little children didn't get the privilege of carrying anything, they wanted hugs instead. We had plenty to go around.

For some reason, Mark and Anna attracted the most children. Maybe it was the love on their faces or perhaps they looked more like the children's big brothers and sisters. I don't know, but it was a beautiful sight. I was so overcome with such a display of love and affection that I completely forgot to take any photos. In the long run I think it was better just to remember it. My mind still carries many clear snapshots that haven't faded in more than 25 years. As we made our way from the plane to the guesthouse the children held our hands, and those who couldn't grasp our hands held on to our pants and shirts. We had to walk very slowly to keep from tripping and falling over the wonderful children. As we left the runway the children's parents also greeted us with joyous words, shaking our hands and smiling. What a welcome!

Included among the Welcoming Party were the minister in the village of Bulape and the doctor from the hospital. They suggested that we take some time to get settled in the guest house, come over to the hospital for a tour, then go to the minister's house for supper. We checked in to the most humble guesthouse I had ever entered. There were hardback chairs in the living room. Each of the three bedrooms had two single beds and a chair in it. There was a commode that occasionally flushed. The windows had no glass or screens. But I have to admit that it was a better accommodation than I thought we might have in a village without any cars.

Heading to the hospital was exciting. After hearing from Keith McCafferty, the Director of the MBF, about the good medical work being done in Bulape we were eager to see it for ourselves. The doctor greeted us at the hospital with all smiles. We knew he was proud of his work and the good work of his staff. I was impressed with the cleanliness of the floors, the bed linens and the uniforms of the nurses. There were no private rooms, only separate wards for the men, the women, and the children. The saddest sights were of the patients with terminal illnesses and also the patients who had significant pain due to insufficient medicine to keep them comfortable. We were glad that we brought an adequate supply of pharmaceuticals to care temporarily for their needs. It was most uplifting to represent Christ to the Bulape people.

After supper at the minister's home we headed back to our guest-house. We were wiped out from our day's stress, excitement and compassion. At the same time we were aware of all the love we had received during the last few hours. The guest house was situated next to a dirt path that was well worn from the foot traffic that headed to and from the hospital. The hospital was no more than 100 yards away. We bathed with a washbasin, soap and cloth by candlelight. That was a first for me, but not the last.

All of us gathered in the living room where Larry had lighted a candle and put it on a chair in the middle of us. We sat in our chairs in a circle. Even in the candlelight you could see the fatigue on our faces, all except for Keith McCafferty's whose face was forever strong and tireless. We sat on our hard back chairs, and at least a few of us wished for a Lazy Boy recliner or a sofa we could curl up on. Larry led us in a discussion of how the day had gone. We ribbed our pilot, Richard, for his "hot dog" flying skills that bordered on acrobatics. He teased us in return for being "city slickers" who couldn't find our own feet without his guidance, much less a small village by plane. Larry led us in a brief devotional using a scripture by memory since the candlelight was too dim to read by. I don't remember the theme of the Bible verses he quoted. All I could think of was my bed, not realizing how hard the mattress was going to be. When our devotional was over I said "Amen" and headed to bed, which must have been stuffed with dried leaves. Mark and Anna stayed up to talk a while.

The hot July evening kept us from sleeping. I lay in bed convinced that there was a sauna in the next room. Even though I was dressed only in shorts and wore no shirt, the sweat beads formed and rolled off my stomach onto the bed. Mark sat on the edge of his bed. We knew that talking about our wish for a ceiling fan would do no good, perhaps make it worse, so we kept our silence. It came to me that the Bulape people experienced these hot and humid conditions every day and I didn't hear any of them complain. So I concentrated on Anne and Julie, wishing they could be on this trip with us. I remember how tired I was, how emotionally exhausted I was too.

I must have fallen asleep but I awakened to the sound of voices in the distance. I pushed the light button on my watch and it read "midnight." What kind of party was it that began so late at night? The singing got louder and closer. I sat up on the side of my bed as the first singer walked down the path by our window with a torch in his hand. He was singing a song like the blues but it had a much sadder tone to it. A second and a third singer processed by the window, One by one, at least twenty-five marchers slowly walked by us. By that time Mark was standing near the window and commented that we were witnessing a wake. Apparently someone had died at the hospital and family and friends were taking the body home. We could hear the eerie cries of the mourners long after they were out of sight. I couldn't sleep again for hours. After 25 years I can still see their faces and hear their wails. It was a night of grief for a Bulape family. We could feel it even though we didn't know the bereaved.

The next morning we toured the hospital with business on our minds. Our main question was how does the Medical Benevolence Foundation best help the hospital to meet its goals for the next year? We learned about the constant need for medicine and supplies such as ether, operating instruments, and a new sterilizer, all things we could provide. But the biggest need was for a children's wing for the hospital. Currently the children were two to a bed in most cases. We agreed to raise the $40,000 to build it and supply it with beds. I was grateful to be a part of MBF and planned to work hard to develop funds for the children's wing during the next year.

The next morning Richard performed more of his amazing flying and swept us skyward from the tiny strip. He made it look easy.

When we got back home in the U.S. we raised the funds for the children's wing. What a privilege! Presbyterians gave generously to make it happen in 1986. The Bulape people still live in my heart today.

Nairobi

In 1985 our team of six flew to Nairobi to visit our medical work there. Our flight from Kinshasa on the west coast of Africa to Nairobi on the east coast took about 7 hours. Thankfully, on this flight there were no chickens hopping about the airplane. Perhaps that was because we were on a Kenyan airline and not the "country bumpkin" Congo airline. This time we were headed for a more modern city than we had seen since Brussels more than a month ago.

Even though we anticipated that the airport was going to be more modern than the ones in Kinshasa, Zaire, it still surprised us to walk off the airplane into a modern terminal that welcomes thousands of tourists annually. There were corridors lined with shops and food vendors. There were several duty free shops selling perfumes and alcohol. Best of all, it was clean. It was a welcomed sight to move up from our third world experience to a second world, even if it was only in the airport and in hotels frequented by tourists. Our plan was to spend three nights in Kenya, the first on R and R at an acceptable hotel in Nairobi, the second at a lodge on a safari a couple of miles from Nairobi, then our third night in the Nairobi hotel prior to our flight back to Brussels, New York and home to Tampa and Clearwater.

On our first day in Nairobi, Keith McCafferty visited Dr. Stan Topple, the medical director in Kikuyu to assess the needs there and to make commitments to him for the year. The rest of the team had the day off to rest and to visit the local shops in the city. The hotel executive warned us to keep our hands on the money in our pockets at all times. Pickpockets were everywhere and very tricky. That advice took away a little of my enjoyment of the shopping visit.

When we returned to the hotel we had lunch and I headed to the pool to relax. A beautiful Kenyan woman sat down on the lounge chair next to mine and offered to meet me in my room for $5. When I declined, she offered to have sex with me for $2. When I told her that I was a Christian and declined her offer another time, she shared that she was a Christian too and that her husband agreed to her being a prostitute because neither of them had job. She stopped by every man at the pool until she found a paying "client." As they walked away toward the hotel, I felt sad to recall that people across the world make a living like she does with sex. The encounter with her only reminded me how ready I was to return to Clearwater with Mark to be with Anne and Julie again.

We got up early the next morning, had a quick breakfast and climbed into our safari mini-bus. Our destination was the Masai Mara and a vast land of animals in the wild. After driving on rough asphalt roads for an hour we headed up a hill on dirt roads that had jaw jarring potholes every 50 feet. I was beginning to think that our time would be better spent swimming in the hotel pool but as we reached the top of the hill, 22 giraffes came bounding across the road in front of us. After sitting in our seats for a long while, suddenly we were up and on our feet with our heads stuck out of the roofless mini-van, gawking like every other tourist in the land. After we got over our shock we began to realize that now was the moment to get out our cameras for some photos. We snapped away. What a moment!

Our safari included sightings of dozens of wildebeests and zebras whose eyes warned us not to get too close. Our last exotic experience was a trip to the river that connects Tanzania with Kenya. As we approached the riverbank our guide reminded us that we would not be allowed outside the vehicle because of the unpredictable nature off hippos. They may come from behind bushes and in fear charge at the bus. Our guide said that more people are killed every year by hippos than lions. That convinced me that inside the bus would be okay by me. Slowly we drove to the edge of the bank where we could see 20 or more hippos bobbing up and down in the river in what looked like family games. Their bellows were so loud that they could be heard for a mile or two. Up river there were more crocodiles than I could count. It was the high point of the safari for me.

Our overnight stay was in a lodge in the middle of the park. Elephants walked all around us at night. Their shrieks were not like the hippos' base voices but they were just as loud. I think that Mark had a good night's sleep but I lay awake much of the night wondering if elephants were going to come lumbering through the lodge. We were up the next morning bright and early to return to Nairobi.

Our last night in Nairobi was a transition from Africa to the U.S. from a world of strange faces to a world of familiar and loving faces, from an impoverished continent to one of wealth. Leaving Kenya felt right. I missed home. I knew that every mile I flew was now another mile closer to home and family.

We didn't have a long layover in Brussels this time but when you're tired of traveling every hour seems too long. As we walked the airport we commented on the drastic difference between the wealthy Brussels airport and the one in Nairobi. Luxurious shops and five star restaurants were available for those with long layovers. From Brussels passengers were traveling to Moscow, Hong Kong, Rome, and of course, New York City.

Our nine-hour flight to New York City was an internally felt, patriotic experience like I'd never had before. When we touched down, I wanted to cheer but instead I just said, "Home again." Keith McCafferty began reciting the Pledge of Allegiance and Mark and I joined in with him. Keith was a 10 on the "life is good" chart. Mark and I said our goodbyes to Keith. He headed back to his home in Houston. Mark and I jumped on our plane to Tampa. We had been gone for four weeks. Touching down in Tampa we scanned the terminal for our two sun-tanned girls. We hugged and kissed like we had been gone for a year. We laughed and cried with the joy of a family that knew love at a deep level. I thought I would never let Anne go. It was great to be home.

Twenty-Five Crying

It was just a few days past Christmas in 1985 when I flew from Clearwater to New York to change planes for Tokyo, Taipei, Bangkok and Dhaka, Bangladesh. Since I was working for the Medical Benevolence Foundation, an arm of the Presbyterian Church that raises funds for medical missionaries around the world, I was on a fact finding trip to learn the needs of doctors, nurses, public health workers, dentists and hospitals where our personnel were in ministry. It was going to be an unforgettable trip. I couldn't wait to meet the missionaries but I wanted to be with the children most of all. I've always had a big heart for kids.

So when I arrived at Kennedy Airport I walked quickly to my gate and was at first thrilled to see approximately 25 Oriental children, ages 5 to 8, waiting to board, along with their nurses. This could be the trip of a lifetime. I hoped that I would be seated near them so that I could interact with them. Then I noticed that all the children had a patch over at least one eye and many of them were crying and obviously in some distress. Suddenly I realized that if I were seated near them that it could turn out be a long, long night flying over the Pacific. My only hope was that the 747 would be big enough to hide me 30 or 40 rows behind the kids. My chances were pretty good. When the boarding began the flight attendants called for the 25 kids and their nurses to board first. The rest of the passengers were patient and understanding of the situation and most of us stayed seated knowing that getting the children settled in their seats would take a little while. I remember feeling sympathetic toward the children, wondering what the circumstances of their eye conditions were.

Finally the rest of us were called to board and with rare excitement I walked down the corridor toward the seat that guaranteed my well-deserved sleep across the Pacific. At the door of the plane the pilot greeted us but the flight attendants were nowhere to be seen. That registered to me as warm and caring since I knew they were busy making the children as comfortable as they could be. So I looked down the aisle and could see that the children were seated, beginning about 10 rows back from first class to ensure that the Gold Card customers wouldn't complain. My seat was going to be somewhere toward the back. Sleep, sweet sleep. But as I passed the children I was jolted by the recognition that I was going to be in an aisle seat right behind the children. Awake, my soul, awake! The rest of the passengers passed by on their way to what I thought must be a bit of heaven. Their noise in putting away their suitcases drowned out most of the kids' crying and I momentarily imagined a quiet cabin.

I was right, the cabin became quiet but it lasted only until the noise of the airplane's take-off thrust cut back after reaching the proper altitude. Then the majority of the children who were feeling badly from eye surgery and also from lack of sleep began to cry and whimper. When one started crying, all of them joined in. I couldn't blame them. I would have been crying too if I were in recovery from having my eye whittled on. However, one thing for sure, our night flight could turn into a nightmare if somebody didn't come up with a plan to help the children adjust to their situation.

A couple of the kids stood up on their seats and looked back at me with the eye that was not patched. I smiled to the best of my ability, knowing it might be the last one I could offer before falling asleep. They smiled back and I broke into a watermelon grin. They ducked down out of sight, then quickly back up and the game was on. The nurses were not totally happy with our game but they were satisfied that these two kids had stopped crying. Little by little the entire row of kids was playing Bob's form of "Duck Duck Goose." Since it was almost 9 P.M. I was ready to try to get some sleep so I waved "night-night" to the row in front, pulled my pillow behind my head, closed my eyes, and pretended to be asleep. I even faked being asleep with rhythmic snoring. It worked. The cabin got quiet.

The noise level kicked up again within 10 minutes. From around the row in front of me peered one of the nurses and with an oriental accent said, "Please Mister, can you do anything else to calm the children?" I was tired enough that I wanted to say, "My fee is $100 an hour." Of course I didn't. So I reached into my bag, pulled out a notebook of 8x11 paper. I stood up so that many of the kids could see me drawing. I drew a dog, a cow, a pig and they all laughed. Then a bird, a giraffe, and a snake and they loved it. Suddenly I became a famous artist. As far as they knew I was Michelangelo's great, great, great grandson. My drawings were actually appreciated by the other adult passengers around us too because now they could get a little sleep. The children settled down and I got some occasional rest. Off and on for the 10-hour trip I had the privilege of reminding the children that their lives were going to be okay soon.

Upon arrival in Tokyo I waved goodbye to the children. Since I had slept very little I could barely think straight enough to find the currency exchange desk to get the money to pay for a bus ride and for the cost of a hotel room. After a 30- minute bus ride I checked into a hotel and went up to my room. At last I could unwind and get some rest. The room was the smallest room I had ever seen in all my life but at least it was a quiet one. I watched TV for a half hour and couldn't settle in so I went downstairs to the lobby to get a bourbon and coke. The elevator door opened and I popped out only to see a sea of Japanese children's faces that lighted up like they had seen Santa Claus. "Yay Mister," they sounded in chorus.

I closed the elevator door as soon as I could and quickly made it back to my third floor cave before the kids could find out which room I was in. When the kids all arrived on my floor with the chatter and whimper I'd grown accustomed to on the jet, I wondered if I would ever get any rest. It started to be another long, restless night but eventually I fell soundly asleep. To this day I don't know who had the servant role, the kids or me. For sure, God had a hand in this first leg of my journey.

Mission Trip To Korea

I worked for the Medical Benevolence Foundation for three and a half years, 1984-1987, between my pastorates in Clearwater and Raleigh. Our organization raised funds for Presbyterian Medical Missions around the world. I went on one of my trips to assess the needs in South Korea, Taiwan, Thailand and Bangladesh from December of 1985 through January of 1986.

South Korea was my main stop. After 16 hours of flying and hanging out in airports I landed in Tokyo where I spent a sleepless night before flying to Seoul, South Korea. I was picked up at the airport by a man who was well-dressed in coat and tie and in his welcome to me he reminded me that the celebration of the 100th anniversary of the Presbyterian Church in South Korea was going to be that evening in the ballroom of the hotel where I would be staying.

Thankfully, I had a couple of hours to shower and dress before I needed to head down to the gathering. As I slipped up the knot on my tie and looked out of my 10th floor window it hit me that Seoul was a metropolis like New York, only larger. The largest Presbyterian Church in the world with more than 100,000 members was in Seoul. They had back-to-back services all day Saturday and from 6 A.M. through 9 P.M. on Sunday in a sanctuary that could seat 5,000. We had large hospitals in Chonju and Kwangju. I had also seen photos of small rural clinics that served primarily the poor. I lay those thoughts aside so that I might finish dressing. I was representing my organization from the U.S. and I needed to join the gathering as soon as possible. So into the elevator I went, acknowledging half-dozen passengers who were dressed to the hilt. I assumed that they were going to hit the town for some entertainment but when the elevator opened they all made their way to the hotel's ballroom.

Entering a lovely ballroom I immediately felt spiritual chills up and down my arms. There were several slide projectors showing many different locations where U.S. missionaries were working faithfully to serve all who were coming to them for healing. But there were also impressive slides of South Koreans doing mission work in other countries. I quickly became aware that I held too narrow of a view of mission work. Christians from Korea were missionaries to other lands also.

There was a banner over the head table: "100 Years For Christ." Perhaps there were as many as 500 men and women talking and laughing. Everyone was drinking what I thought was a South Korean cocktail. When I weaved myself through the elbow-to-elbow crowd and got near the bar I quickly learned that the cocktail being poured for the delight of many was Coca-Cola. I forgot that the South Korean Church was very conservative and frowned on drinking alcohol at any time. Coca-Cola had just recently been introduced into the Orient and was considered more valuable than the finest wines in the U.S. I think it was the Holy Spirit who had expanded the joy in the room. But what surprised me most was how many people in the group spoke English. I was able to speak at least a little with most everyone I met.

The next day I traveled by train to Chonju where I found a 7 floor hospital, supported by Presbyterians in the U.S. and Korea. At that time it was the largest single institution of our mission program in the world. The hospital had 850 staff and saw 14,000 patients each month. Around its work and ministry there was a nursing school, a theology school and a Christian Education school. It was an amazing complex of mission activity. There were many American missionaries in ministry there but the key player was Dr. David Seel who was the Medical Director of the hospital. The missionaries all lived on a compound that housed all 15 families.

The following day I was up early to catch a bus to Kwangju to visit our hospital, plus at least a half dozen more locations of ministry in education and medicine. I heard confidential stories from Rev. Betts Huntley about the 1965 slaughter of hundreds of students who were marching over human rights issues. He spoke these things confidentially in a whispered voice since he would be arrested if overhead and required to leave the country. He told me that the nearby U.S. Air Base knew about the violence and stayed mum. Betts said that in life we have many strange bedfellows. I'd have to agree. We turn our backs on atrocious behavior in the nations where we have military institutions or oil investments.

Sunday was a good day to travel to Soonchun to visit with Clarence and Ruth Durham. They were long time missionaries dedicated to the development of the Wilson Rehabilitation Center that cared for more than 275 men and women at the center and more than 300 in rural clinics. There was a resident at the center who had memorized the entire Bible. Name a chapter and he quickly began to repeat every verse. Astonishing! On Sunday at Dr. Park's (In South Korea, the name Park is like the use of Smith in the U.S.) I enjoyed the most fantastic meal I've ever been served, complete with abalone, shrimp, sea weed, sea cucumbers, chicken, rabbit, squid, octopus, all without forks, only chop sticks. I remember taking a small portion, knowing that it would take me all night to eat with the chopsticks. Everyone humored me and eventually I laughed at myself. Of course, the meal ended with a glass of coke, the prized drink of the South Koreans in the 1980's.

Getting on a train on Monday for Seoul felt good. I wouldn't be on tour for the first time in days. Clarence and I enjoyed a smooth, five-hour ride, arriving mid-afternoon. Since I wasn't to board my next flight to Taipei, Taiwan, until the next morning, we checked into a hotel, went downstairs to a disco, enjoyed a gin and tonic and watched the kids dance to the sounds of Michael Jackson, The Eagles and Charlie Pride. Since half of the population in South Korea is under the age of 25 there is no wonder the house was packed.

When I hit my pillow Monday night I was filled with vivid memories I had accumulated in the Christian ministry in South Korea in less than a week. I wondered if anything could be so impressive on my next stops in Taiwan, Thailand and Bangladesh.

Taiwan Find

On my Orient trip I made a change in plans. Instead of flying to Bang-kok I headed south to Taiwan because I heard of a medical ministry that served hundreds of people every day. My flight was filled with Taiwanese faces but there was one Anglo a couple of rows behind me. When the flight took off and the seat belt sign was off I left my seat and introduced myself. I don't remember her name but she was probably ten years older than I, perhaps in her mid-fifties. I explained the excitement of my first medical mission trip to Taipei. Since there was an empty seat next to her she invited me to sit down and talk with her. She followed with her story of being a Baptist missionary for more than 35 years in a busy city an hour away from Taipei. Her story included the difficulty of being an evangelistic influence in a culture that was partly Buddhist in practice but largely Buddhist by name only. But her narrative included the joys of being heart to heart with so many people over the years. Both of us were enjoying doing God's work in our different ways.

After landing and saying good bye to my Baptist friend, I saw a man at the terminal gate waving his hand toward me with a clipboard and paper on it saying, "Bob Walkup." After warm greetings, David began to chuckle. When I asked him if I had broccoli stuck between my teeth or egg on my shirt he just laughed easily and said, "You'll see." But in the meantime we traveled slowly in the hospital car through Taipei, the busiest city I had ever seen, including New York City. There were plenty of cars on the go but there were hundreds of mopeds clogging every street and intersection. David told me that 40% of the patients at the hospital where he worked were treated for bike accidents.

As we neared the hospital where the Presbyterian Missionaries worked he thought it was time to have some lunch. We pulled into the only parking place in front of a small, one-room apartment upstairs and an equally small kitchen on the bottom floor. There was one table near the street. I think it was the most unremarkable restaurant I'd ever seen in my life. But I just kept quiet. David would likely go out of his way to welcome a first timer to Taiwan so I decided to let him do the talking.

As we sat down at the single table I wondered about David's choice of restaurants. When a man came to the table with an apron around his waist I assumed he was the waiter but I learned he was the owner of the house, the kitchen, the dining area and that he was also the chef. David explained that he had eaten in Taipei in the expensive restaurants and in the more affordable ones, but that a friend of his told him about the tasty meals in this unpretentious place. David held up two fingers and the chef smiled and went to work in a wok and stirring in a small pot. In 10 minutes the chef brought us a bowl of wonton and a bowl of chicken and noodles that surpassed any dish served to me in the U.S. In the middle of our meal David remembered that we had forgotten to give thanks for our food and so we bowed our heads while he said a simple but bountiful prayer.

We finished our meal and jumped into the hospital car. After dodging bikes for 30 minutes we arrived at a modern looking hospital. David began to chuckle again and I begged him to tell me what was going on. He said, "You'll see very soon now." We entered the front door and climbed the steps to the second floor. As we walked onto the hallway I could see at least a dozen nurses and orderlies carrying out their duties from room to room. That's when David said, "Get ready, your surprise is coming down the hallway."

I stopped in my tracks. I couldn't believe my eyes. Perhaps I was seeing double. Maybe I had been flying too many hours and needed more rest. A doctor in a white coat approached me and broke into a smile of delightful surprise. So did I. David said, "Now you see why I've been chuckling for more than an hour." Coming towards me was a man that looked more like me than I did. His height and weight were like mine. Had I missed something in my family tree? Was I a twin who was separated from his brother in my early childhood?

As the unknown identical twin and I shook hands, David quietly said, "Bob Walkup, I'd like to introduce you to Bob Walkup." In silence I smiled over the serendipity of the moment. We shook hands warmly, and then had the urge to hug one another. Backing away from our embrace I felt a tear running down my face. We moved to his office and learned that we both had the name Robert Harvey Walkup, a name too rare to be anything but family. I learned that he was a Jr. and that his Dad was also Robert Harvey Walkup, a Presbyterian minister in Mississippi. I had heard about the Mississippi Walkups long before this time, but I had never had any contact with them. The doctor and I learned that we were third cousins who had traveled 12,000 miles to meet. We enjoyed being with each other several more times before I left for Bangkok and Changmai. But when I returned to the U.S. I paid a visit to Preacher Bob in his summer home in Montreat, N.C. Needless to say, our family resemblance was quite strong. Genetics tell the truth.

Bangkok, Buddha and Bob

I wasn't ready to leave Taiwan. Meeting the "other" Bob Walkup gave me a sense of familiarity in a strange land. There is something about meeting an old friend or a relative half way around the world that transforms it from just a strange place to a bit of home, if only briefly. David drove me to the airport and wished me well. It had been a quick but helpful, two-night stay in Taipei.

My five-hour flight to Bangkok, the capital of Thailand, was quiet, no passengers talking loudly, no children crying, just smooth and easy. Perhaps it was preparation for what I was about to find in Bangkok. When the door of the plane opened and I walked down the steps to the tarmac my throat quickly began to dry out. I was too excited to make too much of it so I walked through the airport doors expecting something good. The crowd was packed into the terminal like sardines in a can and everyone was moving, shoving, bumping into one another but without apparent short-tempered bursts of anger like I had seen in the U.S. metropolitan terminals over the years. But it meant that claiming my duffle bag was more like running an obstacle course. And I had been warned about pickpockets rifling through whatever they could unzip and be gone in seconds with something of real value, such as my camera or important film. Certainly I needed to keep my wallet and passport at the bottom of my camera case for safety and quick retrieval.

It was no small relief to make it to the pick-up zone. Immediately I understood why my throat had gone dry when leaving the plane. Billows of blue smoke were drifting across the terminal parking lot from the exhausts of dozens of taxis. Pollution control obviously was a rejected idea in Thailand. I looked around at the disturbing sight. All of the cabbies were fighting for the privilege of taking you the 20 miles into Bangkok. Each offered me "the cleanest, fastest, most enjoyable ride into town." I jumped into the one closest to me that had the worse paint job, thinking that the exterior of his cab might indicate he'd been around a long time and might have better experience as a driver. The Thai cabs were motorized rickshaws. You might call them motorbikes with room enough for two in back in a small cage.

The driver spoke English well enough to understand exactly where I wanted to go. The traffic moved dangerously fast on the three lanes towards the city. The cabs all drove at least 50 mph with each vehicle just a few feet apart. Waves of black and blue exhausts shrouded my cab. I couldn't see more than 200 feet ahead. When I expressed my anxiety over the trip the driver guaranteed me safe travel, saying that he'd made this trip thousands of times. The way he weaved in and out of traffic without a fatal wreck had me believing he was telling the truth. So I resigned myself to putting a handkerchief over my nose to cut the noxious fumes, wondering how the Thai people make it from day to day.

After an hour we arrived at The Christian Guest House, a way station for travelers. It was unimpressive on the outside. When I entered the front door the middle-aged manager greeted me warmly but with an air of objectivity, perhaps due to his role in ushering so many people in and out of the house every week. No need to get close. He showed me to my bedroom. I was going to sleep in a single bed with only room enough to stand beside it. There was a folding chair and a small chest for my bags. The community bath was down the hall. For $7 a night I couldn't ask for much more.

I learned that supper would be served in a half hour so I washed my face and hands and walked to the den to meet a dozen men and women in the lounge. They were from all over the world, from Europe and Asia, Africa and the United States. Our conversation went from ministry to family to sports. It was lively and enjoyable. At supper we all sat around one long table. I had a feeling of what it might be like when we get to heaven. People from all races gathered together around one table. After a decent meal we retired to the living room where we told family stories until my droopy eyes signaled bedtime. My bed was hard and my pillow lumpy but I decided that the privilege of being in Thailand left no reason for complaint.

The next morning after breakfast I asked if anyone wanted to go with me to visit The Reclining Buddha. A woman in her 30's agreed. Catherine was from the UK and had a dry sense of humor. We walked to a nearby river and hopped into a motorboat that looked like a long motorized canoe with a driver. After a half hour's ride we climbed on to land and walked a block to our destination. There he was, The Reclining Buddha, one hundred feet long, twenty-five feet high, painted in gold. Impressive. More impressive were the 5 priests who sat nearby inhaling Winston cigarettes. Since I had studied about Buddhism before the trip I asked if they believed that it was important to extinguish cravings so that no passion remained. When they agreed I asked if smoking was not a craving. They agreed again but indicated that smoking was not a major offense to their beliefs. Our lively conversation lasted for an hour or so. I thought about how Christians also rationalize our beliefs to suit our behavior.

On the way back to the guesthouse we passed Sin City. Dozens of stores and lounges with scantily dressed women at the doors invited us in to enjoy sex. My friend and I were in disbelief over the openness and lawlessness of sexual behavior in Bangkok. It was an "anything goes" ethic. Now I could understand why the favorite place of furlough for the soldiers in the War in Vietnam was Bangkok. They could find everything they desired and more. Morality flew out of the window. We also learned that the young women and girls in the sex shops were probably lied to by sex traders into thinking that they were going to be taken from their impoverished homes in Cambodia, Burma and Vietnam in order to receive an education in a fine school in Bangkok. They were caught in slavery until they were too old or sick with STD's to perform in the sex shops. I felt an acute pain in my stomach and I wanted to rush in and try to save a few girls from their enslavement but I could see that their managers were packing pistols in clear view.

Obviously there was an illusion in Bangkok that sex can satisfy the soul. But when I remembered the porn industry in the U.S. I had to drop a portion of my American self-righteousness. I don't think that God intended the good creation of sex to lose its sacredness and be distorted into the secular den of iniquity I was witnessing. Apparently all I could do was to pray for the girls to be freed to go home again.

My friend and I returned to the guesthouse and discussed what we had seen with a few of the travelers in the living room. Each of us tried to soothe our souls by talking about the good work we were doing in Thailand. I shared my work for the next two days, which was to fly to Chang Mai, a city in northern Thailand where we have a Presbyterian hospital and a Leprosy Community.

Changmai Surprise

When I left the noisy metropolis Bangkok for a city in northern Thailand I had been told that I would be going to a city totally different from anything I'd seen on my trip up to that point. I was really ready for the change. So when the plane lifted off the runway I leaned back in my chair and tried to imagine what was in store for me in Changmai. I had been told that the hospital was modern and that our missionary doctor was a delightful fellow. When we landed a driver from the hospital picked me up at the airport and casually drove me through a well-ordered city. It was a far cry from the noisy metropolis of Bangkok. The temperature went from Bangkok's 90 degrees to a comfortable 75 degrees. It was hilly and lush in vegetation. Everything was green. The trees were huge and draped casually over the roads and streams. For a minute I thought I was in the mountains near Montreat, N.C.

Our car pulled into the hospital parking lot. The hospital was large and had a reputation for being the finest in the country. My driver guided me to the office of the missionary physician, whose name escapes me, and he warmly welcomed me. After initial greetings he toured me through the hospital and was very proud of the hospital's reputation. I could see why. It was immaculate and the medical teams seemed to be caring and efficient in their ministry to the patients. As we walked he would point out the needs of the hospital and itemize those things that needed immediate attention. I was inspired by him and felt determined to work to fill those needs when I returned to the U.S.

We then walked to his home, which was on the campus. After a rest we gathered in his dining room where his wife and cooks served us a traditional Thai dinner. Not having eaten a traditional meal I dived into the dishes that were both sweet and sour. The chicken and vegetables tasted delicious, that is, until the hot spices began to work their way into my cheeks and tongue. Tears began running down my face and my nose ran like a garden hose. I didn't want to insult the host or cooks so I kept eating and crying through the entire meal. When the cooks offered me seconds I politely obliged and ate my fill. Every so often I would look up at the doctor and his wife who were more than amused at my eating experience. I kept waiting for someone to bring me some water with ice but ice was not a part of the culture. When the meal was over and our evening conversation ended I returned to my room and spent the next hour drinking water to put out my oral fire. That meant that I was up most of the night going to the bathroom. Oh well, it was worth it. Like Dr. Seuss' character says,"Oh, the places you'll go and the people you'll see."

The next morning I visited the most uplifting place I've ever been. I was told that on the hospital campus there was a special village that I would not want to miss. So the doctor walked with me from his home to a building that was filled with people, not unlike me, in some ways. But as I walked closer to the people I could see that the men and women had only nubs for fingers. Their faces were shaped like people who had been in a terrible accident. Most of them had also lost the toes on both feet. I was in a village of people with leprosy. It was shocking for me at first. But as the doctor talked with them they began to laugh and talk as normally as anyone did. Their harmonica band was uplifting with its lovely songs. The most fascinating thing I learned was that they had developed a profitable trade painting beautiful scenes from their town, using only the nubs of their fingers to do the work. No one was feeling sorry for themselves. They were using what they had to benefit the community. They lived together, played together, and they worshiped together. There was a spirit of acceptance there that beat anything I'd ever witnessed. There was a love shared among them that built up one another and made each person feel like a brother or sister.

I left Changmai feeling proud of our excellent hospital but I remember the people in the Leprosy Village with great thanksgiving. I still have a hard time feeling sorry for myself.

Bangladesh Faces

I stepped down from the airplane on a hot July morning in 1985 onto the hot tarmac in Dhaka, Bangladesh. I had traveled with a plane full of mostly Bengali faces. Perhaps there were also many passengers from neighboring countries including India, Burma, Thailand, and Nepal but I couldn't tell the difference. It looked like I was a distinct minority of one. One thing for sure, they knew I was a stranger in their midst. I had the only white face among the 75 or so people who had made the flight from Bangkok to Dhaka and I stood out in the crowd like a zebra among a herd of gazelles.

As I walked into the terminal I was stopped by customs agents with rifles who channeled me into a small cubicle with my duffle bag and my camera bag that I carried over my shoulder. I spoke in English to several agents who ignored my attempt to communicate with them. A half hour later one of them approached me and opened my bag. He pulled out everything on to a table, sifted through my belongings, a pair of pants, 2 pairs of underwear, 2 shirts, a pair of new sandals that I bought in Bangkok just for this occasion, and a small personal bag with a toothbrush, toothpaste, shampoo and a small scissors to trim my beard. He took my scissors and my shampoo without explanation and I wasn't about to ask him why. As far as I was concerned he could keep most anything there but my underwear. He then left and talked for another half hour with the other agents.

When the customs agent returned he began emptying my camera case of all its contents. First he pulled out my new Ricoh camera and held it up to the light, then toward the other agents who all grinned like they were at a birthday party. Then he took my telescopic lens and did the same routine. I knew he was going to take them away so I quickly said, "If you speak English I'd like to tell you something." He looked quickly at me and then I knew he did. I offered to take a picture of him and his men and immediately he smiled and nodded yes. I stood as they gathered by their desk and I took a half dozen photos of them to their delight. Then he looked over the other contents, especially my notebook full of information about hospitals and clinics in Korea, Taiwan, and Thailand. When I explained that I was a doctor's helper his suspicion seemed to subside. When he told me to pack up my things and go I did just as I was told before he could change his mind. I thought he would keep my camera but he handed it back to me. I was so appreciative that I bowed to the agents like they were royalty.

Leaving customs and moving into the terminal was like swimming up a fast flowing river. Hundreds of people, mostly men, were shoulder to shoulder, jumping up and down trying to get the attention of passengers exiting the next plane. Since I didn't see a white face in the crowd I knew that I had to push my way through the crowd like other passengers were doing. It was like a scrum in rugby, everyone pushing to get an advantage for themselves.

Finally an hour and a half later I saw one of our missionaries, Craig Meisner, who pulled me through the logjam to his van. I was frazzled but happy. We pulled out of the airport in his van and immediately hit a bottleneck of rickshaws, makeshift shops by the roadsides, and hundreds of people on every block. I had been in problematical jams in Bangkok but it was nothing like Dhaka. It took us two hours to go five miles to his home. To make things worse, there were military guards at every intersection, stopping cars and rickshaws and looking for weapons or other illegal items of every kind. There had been a riot the day before and nine people had been killed and hundreds injured. The news that Martial Law was in effect somehow made me feel safer. My visit seemed even more important than before.

Arriving at Craig's home in Dhaka was wonderful. It seemed more like home to me than the homes I visited in Japan, Korea, Taiwan, and Thailand. The conversation and the food suited my needs. The only irritating thing was the extremely loud call to prayer that screamed over the loudspeakers in every neighborhood. I'll have to admit, however, that Christians are missing out daily on the privilege of regular prayer times.

The next day I had the privilege of meeting the Bangladesh church leaders in Dhaka. The most impressive understanding I walked away with was the law that prohibited evangelism in public. Offenders are jailed. The ministry, therefore, was growing slowly but it also seemed to be maturing. When we later visited our public health work north of Dhaka in the Tongi area I felt proud to be a Presbyterian. Over a thousand patients were being seen in our clinic every week. The lines of people who came for medical help remained long from morning until closing time at night.

The most challenging part of my entire trip was yet to come. Our Dhaka missionary, Craig, carried me to the nearest port on the Ganges River, bought me a ticket on a ferry, and waved goodbye. I knew that Scott Smith, our community development missionary in the southern region, was going to meet me, but when I shoved off with 150 others I knew that the ferry couldn't have been made for more than 100. I felt like I was on Humphrey Bogart's famous African Queen, just a larger version. We were obviously listing on the port side. I prayerfully remembered stories of the frequent capsizing of ferries on the Ganges. Eventually the captain must have asked the passengers to move because when the captain spoke over the loudspeaker everyone took a step to the right and the boat balanced itself. All of the passengers did the Bengali One Step dance a half dozen times as we made our way down stream in a seductive current.

Everyone was standing as close as bees in a hive. I could easily tell that Bangladesh had too little money for food and none for deodorants. When I thought I was the only one on the ferry that spoke English a man standing nearby asked me, "Do you know J.R. in Dallas?" He caught me by surprise! I did my best to explain the difference between a TV show and reality but I could tell by the expression on his face that I failed.

The trip across the dangerous Ganges River took only about an hour. The river which is wider than the Mississippi overflows its banks two or three times every year, sweeping away thousands of people and two thirds of the nation's rice crop with them.

I couldn't be happier to see Scott Smith waving from the rickety dock. When I waved back to Scott many of the passengers waved along with me. Maybe my brief conversation with the Bengali man had been more successful than I knew. Scott and I hugged each other like we were brothers even though we had never seen each other before. On a spiritual level we were brothers in Christ. My time with Scott and his family turned out to be some of the most formative and thought provoking days of my entire pilgrimage.

Crossing The Ganges River

When I was a guest at Craig Meisner's home in the capital of Dhaka, Bangladesh I thought I had seen the poorest of the country's poor, but when I stepped down from the ferry that took me across the Ganges River my heart was touched by the thousands of people who lacked the basics of life. Scott Smith met me at the ferry and since there were no cars in that part of the country he gave my duffle bag to a man to carry it for me. I initially felt saddened for the man because he was so small and thin. I thought I should be carrying my own things. I was in much better health than he was. The people needed food and clean water, a roof over their heads and a job to earn a living. But they had none of these. Perhaps some of them had food earlier in the year but floodwaters had washed away their crops for the third time during the last 12 months.

I walked with Scott Smith through the hordes of faces that crowded around us. There were at least 500 men, women, and little children following us, enveloping us like a cocoon. The women lagged behind in their subservient way. People looked at us, hopeful for a handout or for anything that might sustain them for one more day. I remember one young man, about 20 years old, who kept tapping my camera bag with his hand. I thought he probably was looking for food so I unzipped my bag, pulled out my camera, and let him look inside the empty space. All of the people then looked at my camera and Scott told me that they were wondering what it was so I pulled out my photo of Anne, Mark and Julie and held it by the camera. Some of the people understood but the majority of them had never seen a camera before and were puzzled by it all. So Scott explained it the best he could. His knowledge of the language must have been adequate because the people stopped begging me for food.

When we had walked about an hour down a narrow path we arrived at Scott and Melanie's home. They had two young daughters. The Smiths lived in a very small village where about a dozen families lived in traditional housing. Because the Smiths lived in solidarity with the people, they lived in housing just like ones the Bengali families lived in. They had a roof of thatch and mud over a dirt floor. Their beds were pallets laid out on dirt that was built up six inches off the ground. Since there was no electricity or running water, they cooked over wood fires and boiled their water from a nearby muddy pool. They had no commode so they had to care for their sanitation needs like people did in the U.S. in the 1800's.

The Smith's showed me to my room that was just a part of the living room with a curtain drawn. Whatever anyone did or said could be heard by everyone else in the small home. It was primitive. During the two days I was with the Smiths I never got used to it. I did, however, grow in my appreciation for the Smiths who could have chosen to live in more modern accommodations. Since they were doing community development in hopes of training families how to live together and support one another, the Smiths strongly felt that living like the people lived was necessary if their instruction was going to be effective.

An hour down the road by foot, Dr. and Mrs. Nonweiler ran a medical clinic that served people who would walk all day for help. Some would carry a sick friend for many miles to help him get well. It was a great service. The Nonweilers also worked with a nurse who came from Dhaka and was as dedicated to the ministry as they were. My two days in their home and assisting in the clinic convinced me that our missionaries were going the extra mile to serve Christ. But my observations at their clinic and in all of the mission stations where I visited impressed me with the very high level of stress they lived under. The demand for their services, whether they were for medical, community development, church development, or simply friendship, was greater than what the missionaries had to give. They felt isolated. The Presbyterian Mission Board in Louisville would send a letter only every 6 months. They wondered if anyone really appreciated them.

Later in the week I made my way back across the Ganges River to Dhaka and prepared to fly toward home in Florida. But as I expressed some of my concerns about the emotional hardships I saw in the missionary team the project manager asked if I would return to help them manage those concerns. I promised I would.

Six months later I returned to Dhaka to do a spiritual renewal week with the five couples on the team. I helped them re-affirm their faith in Christ as Lord of their mission. But just as important, I provided a workshop on marriage enrichment each day. It was one of the most gratifying weeks of my life. While our time together didn't make their work easier it renewed their understanding and appreciation of each other.

Our missionaries in Bangladesh served valiantly. But they didn't serve long in their stations. The cultural shock and stress brought their mission work to a close before their plans could be fully implemented. Two of the couples went through divorces shortly afterwards.

Today, as I look back, I remember our denomination asking me in 1987 to return to Bangladesh to be the project manager to oversee the ministry there. I considered it only briefly. My mind was too filled with stressful stories from that part of the world. The Spirit aimed me in another direction, specifically to the Saint Andrews Presbyterian Church in Raleigh, N.C. The request to go to the Saint Andrews Church came the day after the denomination asked me to go to Bangladesh. God's interesting timing!

A New Path

Saint Andrews' Holy Call

God is always in the business of directing our paths. Some paths are troubling when God seems to be out of touch with us. Other paths are exciting and joyful. God seems as close as the nose on our faces. We would bet our lives on the faith that we're walking a holy path with God as our leader. My call to Saint Andrews Presbyterian in Raleigh in 1987 was one of those times when I could clearly see God at work in my life, and in the lives of Anne, Mark, and Julie as well.

I enjoyed my ministry with the Medical Benevolence Foundation for three and a half years from 1984 to 1987. My highest accolades, then and still today, go out to our missionaries because their dedicated ministry in the name of Christ is remarkable. Their work under some of the most difficult situations imaginable showed me the power of the Holy Spirit like I had never witnessed before. But halfway into my fourth year with MBF I found myself getting very tired, sleeping poorly, finding it hard to leave home for another four days of travel. I began to feel uninspired when I stood to preach or to make a presentation to a church. I was deeply committed to the world mission work of our denomination but I began to feel a shift in God's call to me.

A fascinating thing began to happen. I started having a recurring dream, the first on New Year's Day in 1987. The dream would reoccur when I was in various places, in Jacksonville, Orlando, Tallahassee, Tampa, Brandon, Daytona Beach, and also when I was at home in Clearwater. In the dream I was the pastor of a red brick church in North Carolina with a caution light blinking at a nearby crossroad. The town was Delmar. I looked up that town in a map and it wasn't listed. But the dream got my attention. I began asking God if this was the symbol of a church where I might become the pastor. After 3 or

4 months of dreaming about the red brick church in North Carolina I was prepared for anything. I was prepared but the phone didn't ring.

One Sunday night in June, I preached in a church near Cape Kennedy. I was tired as I headed home to Clearwater on a back road called the Beeline Highway. It was ten o'clock at night and I was thinking about how good it would be if I could get on a God-powered rocket and head to a new call, preferably to a church. I asked God to give me something to let me know that my dreaming and praying was on track. Within minutes I had to slow down my car because there were three deer in the road, immobilized by my headlights. Since it was such a deserted part of the highway, I parked the car, got out, went within 20 feet of the deer, and talked to them like I was Noah gathering passengers for the next ark. There were no other cars passing by to spook them so we enjoyed one another's presence for at least 10 minutes before I returned to the car and drove around them. My Noah experience with the deer sent chills up and down my spine. I spent the night in Orlando and headed back to Clearwater the next morning.

It was to be one of the most uplifting days of my life. The phone did ring. As a matter of fact, three times it rang. The first call was from our Mission Board in Louisville asking if I would become the pastor of our ministry in Bangladesh. I replied that I didn't feel God's call to international mission work at that time. The phone rang a second time and it was the chair of the pastor nominating committee in Mississippi, asking me to consider being their pastor. Again I said no without any apparent reason. The Spirit said no.

Then later in the afternoon, I got a call from Sylvia Norman asking me to consider being the pastor of the Saint Andrews Presbyterian Church in Raleigh, North Carolina. Immediately my spiritual ears perked up. I asked quickly if the church was red brick and Sylvia said yes. I swallowed hard, did my best to collect myself, and with great confidence told Sylvia that I had been waiting for a phone call from North Carolina and I agreed to be considered. Since I didn't have my PIF completed, (Personal Information Form), I agreed to complete it and to send it to them right away. Within a few days I received a call from Pat McInnes, a member of the search committee, who wanted to discuss additional ideas. Before the week was out I had mailed a tape of one of my sermons to Raleigh. The week was a whirlwind of the Holy Spirit for Anne and me.

After Anne and I visited Saint Andrews in late June the committee offered me the position. Anne agreed it was God's doing. We committed to moving to Raleigh in July. But Julie didn't see the Call including her. She wanted to stay in Clearwater for her senior year with her good friend, Nikki. We agreed and she made her plans to stay. Mark was at USC so the move didn't cause as great a concern for him. But after a few weeks Julie tearfully told us that her heart had been changed and that she was going with us to Raleigh. Anne and I were thrilled. All of the pieces of our spiritual puzzle were in place. Perhaps the best moment in all of our thinking about my Call was the first afternoon we arrived in Raleigh when Anne, Julie, and I walked into the original, small sanctuary. It was Julie's first time to enter the sanctuary. We opened the door, walked in without a word and stood in the worshipful sunlight beaming through the yellow glass. Within moments Julie had tears rolling down her cheeks. It was the right place and she was moving with us to Saint Andrews.

The last piece of the puzzle was the blinking, caution light. I dropped that piece out of my mind. All the other pieces of God's puzzle were in place and I didn't expect everything to perfectly fit. But after the

222

first worship service we went home for lunch and lay down for a nap. I woke up almost startled and told Anne that the last piece of the puzzle was at the top of our subdivision, a caution light less than a mile from the church. And I'm told that the light was not there when I began my dreaming. It had been hung only a month before we arrived.

The days leading up to my Call to Saint Andrews were among the most astounding days of my entire life. Those days constantly remind me that God's plan is both visible and invisible, spiritually audible and spiritually hushed. That's our God!

Craig Holladay

When I had been the Pastor of the Saint Andrews Presbyterian for a short while it became clear that we needed help to provide additional leadership for our growing congregation. The Search Committee and I plowed through more than a hundred job applications, interviewed two candidates and virtually threw up our hands in despair. Nobody we looked at could come close to matching our needs for another pastor. After months of work and prayer we wondered how God would fill our needs. Then one afternoon Craig Holladay called to explore the possibility that we might enjoy working together in ministry. From our conversation I knew that the Holy Spirit was moving among us. He sent us his resume' which we poured over looking for a potential problem he might bring with him. There was one; he was graduating from Fuller Seminary, which is an interdenominational seminary. Would his theological understanding of God and the church be too conservative for Presbyterians? We invited Craig for a visit.

He flew in from California and when I saw his face I believed he was the one. After he answered a few questions before the Search Committee I knew he was the one. Now it was just a matter of thoroughly interviewing him. We quickly discovered that he was highly intelligent, a dedicated Christian man, an articulate speaker, and perhaps best of all, Craig's humor and laughter were contagious. Before the committee voted I knew the outcome. His call to Saint Andrews was unanimous. The church felt the blessing he brought immediately. Craig's love for Christ was never doubted. His preaching impressed the congregation and me, even though he was fresh out of school. His teaching was organized and challenging.

Over the 11 years that we worked together I discovered that I was not the primary leader in the church but only one of the two. Craig was the other. I know that I gave him my leadership but Craig gave me his energy and creative ideas. We were a team in the highest sense of the word. Though I was his senior by many years I realized that his devotional approach to life had made him stronger than his years. I loved working with him. Whether we were in a staff meeting, a Session meeting or a worship service, we often knew what the other was thinking, a gift of the Spirit for our work together. Perhaps our leadership in worship displayed our togetherness more than at any other time. Craig always knew how to supplement my needs and I his. My years in ministry with Craig were my most fulfilling. He is a God-gifted man.

When I developed a late onset of bipolar disorder in 1999, I resigned with great sadness. Craig's leadership was strong and all the church needed. He had all the gifts necessary to bring the congregation through the crisis. When the Presbytery denied him the privilege of being the senior pastor it disturbed the congregation greatly. The Presbytery had promised me two years previous that they would make an exception if I should leave my position for any reason. The Presbytery had set the precedent for another church in Durham that was not going through a crisis at all. The result was harsh. The wounds were deep. Craig left the Presbyterian Church and created a new church called Grace Community Church. More than half the members followed Craig. It left Saint Andrews with a big debt to manage and the members who stayed were angry. But all things considered, Craig followed his understanding of God's will.

Craig did Spirit-led work at Grace until he began experiencing significant stress and neck pain from an earlier injury. It gradually rendered him less effective than the elders required in a Senior Pastor. Craig's health has continued to decline for a few years. He's been through multiple, dangerous surgical procedures on his neck without any healing. Craig's health has prevented him from being in active ministry. It saddens him, as it does many of us who have been blessed by his Christian love and dedicated service. Nevertheless, he is spiritually sound and a joy to be around.

Craig is a dear brother of mine. In my years of ministry I name Craig as one of the most gifted pastors of all.

Tornado

It was April of 1988. At our home in Raleigh, NC, Anne and I listened to the wind howl and heard the tree limbs cracking in the strong wind. It was in the middle of the night so we cuddled up closer and decided that the morning would be soon enough to see what the storm had brought us. The ferocious sounds of the night traveled away as fast as they came. We fell back asleep. About 6 A.M. Mike Bruton called and said, "Bob, you need to come down to the church right away." I quickly dressed, walked out of the door, jumped into my car and backed out of the garage. I hadn't gone 10 feet before I saw the reason Mike had called. There was half of a rooftop lying in our front yard. It had severed the tops out of many of our pines as it sailed from the sky towards our home. I rushed around the house to see if there was damage to our home and was relieved to see that there was none. Pines had fallen all over our property but none of them had damaged our home. Anne and I celebrated that our home was spared but immediately we thought about the home whose roof was in our front yard. How bad was it for our neighbors and had the church been damaged badly?

So down the driveway and up to Falls of Neuse Road we drove, dodging the trees and home materials that had been strewn across the road. I had experienced tornadoes in Clearwater so I knew what I was heading towards. My heart felt heavy as I looked at the damage to many neighborhoods along the way. Since Mike's words had offered a sound of deep concern I was afraid to see what our Saint Andrews Presbyterian Church looked like. When I turned into the church driveway I could only go a few feet before I had to stop my car.

In front of me lying on the ground were almost all of the pine trees on our property. It was a tangled mess of "pick-up-sticks." I feared the worse, unlike a man of faith. But Mike toured me around the property, showing me that the building was untouched, even though 164 trees had fallen all around it. Not one had hit Saint Andrews. Some of us gathered on the front circle and held hands as we prayed. Some of us thanked God for sparing us from the troubles that we knew other folks around us were experiencing. Others of us prayed for guidance so that we would know how to be servants for the huge number of families around us whose homes were badly damaged.

We didn't have to look far to offer our help. The Baptist Church next door to us had its sanctuary roof blown away. We shared our sanctuary with them for many months while their building was repaired. Many neighborhoods lost their homes so we helped with meals, chainsaws, hammers, electrical wiring, skill saws, baby sitting and counseling. We invited neighbors to worship with us and they did. The most astounding fact about the tornado is that there were no deaths and only a few injuries. It was the nearest thing to a miracle that I've ever witnessed.

Now I wonder why God had a reason to spare the Presbyterians and not the Baptists next door that morning. It certainly wasn't because one was more righteous than the other, or that one had a preacher needing a greater challenge than the other. Life brings us all kinds of unplanned events that cause us to think seriously about God's will for the world and our lives.

Honestly, I can never understand in life why one baby is born healthy and one is born with a handicap. I don't understand why one soldier dies in Iraq and the other lives when their truck is struck by a roadside bomb. I don't comprehend why a gifted T.V. broadcaster who is a strong Christian here in our city is struggling with a terminal brain tumor. It isn't apparent to me, even after 10 years, why my bipolar disorder bucked me right out of the saddle in my prime. I had great plans for my future in the church but my illness stopped me rudely without warning.

From a human perspective life is haphazard and without reasonable planning on God's part. It spares the evil ones and takes down the good servants without apparent cause. It looks as if God is both cruel and unjust with all people everywhere. Yet without long discussions on the will of God we can by faith say with Job (J0b 42) "Lord, I know you can do all things, and that no purpose of yours can be stopped." Job's faith is mine. God's power and love is able to do all things. God's work is often unseen or misunderstood, so by faith we live our lives through the sunshine and the rain.

God is working with us in our present to understand our past and our future. Often I don't see God's hand but like Paul we can say, "In everything God works for good for everyone who loves him." (Romans 8:28).

A tornado brings out the worse and best in us. It presses our faith to its limits. In North Raleigh there is a clear sign along the roadways that points to trust in God.

Waffle House Martha

When I was the minister at the Saint Andrews Church I visited Richmond, Virginia twice a year to develop my preaching and worship plan for the next six months. It was May of 1990 and my destination was Union Presbyterian Theological Seminary where I could find old and new resources to read. But the study areas in the library were uncomfortable with upright chairs and since my back surgeries had left me with the need to find a comfortable place to study, I looked on my first trip to Richmond for a clean motel with a reasonable rate.

Three hours later I found what I had been looking for, a humble, 12-room motel managed by an Indian couple on the Southside of town, approximately fifteen minutes from the campus. I might have chosen other motels near the school but there were no restaurants near them. Thankfully, this Eastern Motel had a comfy chair to read in and it was in the vicinity of seven or eight restaurants within a mile, all in walking distance, which I needed to do anyway.

There was a Pizza Hut, a Red Lobster, Mary's Family Restaurant and a Papa John's take out pizza place on the other side of the street from my motel. On my side of the street were the Thai Village, a Subway, and an S&S Cafeteria at the mall. There also was a Waffle House that was just two doors down from my motel.

I checked in to the Eastern Motel, took a half hour nap and headed back to Union Seminary to check out approximately 20 books that I wanted to read or research. After a few hours I had found and checked out the material I wanted and drove back to the motel. I had two queen beds so I spent a couple of hours flipping through each book and placing them on the bed in specific categories including worship, mission, education, management, personal growth, and spirituality. It was time for supper so I walked to the Subway for a sandwich. The mall was just up the road so after I ate my sub I made my way there and had a relaxing time checking out the stores. I decided to return to the mall another day and maybe have a meal in the food court. Everything smelled so good, even after I had already eaten.

I walked back toward my motel and halfway there I saw four young black men coming in my direction. I felt highly aware of my surroundings and planned my escape route if I needed to flee from a potential conflict. When we got closer they all moved to the side of the walkway to let me go by and one of them greeted me courteously. I knew immediately that I still harbored a prejudice against African Americans, even though I'd worked all my life to see each one with positive thoughts. Back at the motel my first day was closing. I was tired from the transition from Raleigh to Richmond. It was early but I went to bed without setting a clock. I would get up the next morning only when I naturally woke up. Monday would be a good day to get serious for the week's study.

I was surprised to find that it was already 9:30 A.M. when I drew the curtains back to let the sunshine in. After 12 hours of sleep I had actually caught up with myself. I felt restored. I also wanted some coffee right away so I pulled a pair of jeans on and an old sweatshirt and walked pass a couple of stores to the Waffle House. I pulled the door open to the smell of grits, eggs and bacon. There was obviously the wonderful drift of waffles and maple syrup floating my way too. Before I could get the door closed a high voice rang out, "Good morning stranger, welcome to the Waffle House, my name is Martha, what's yours?" I guess I hesitated for a minute, wondering if I was still dreaming back at the motel. By the time I faced reality Martha's voice rang out again, "Don't be afraid to tell us your name, we'll all friends here." I stumbled out a "Bob" and the whole crowd said, "Good morning Bob." So I bravely ushered a "Good morning," in return.

Martha practically ushered me to a seat at the counter and sounded out a "coffee for Bob coming right up." I took my seat between two fellows, one my age, around 50 or so, and the other man sitting on my right, a retired man in his early 70's who said to me, "Welcome to the Waffle House, you might be a stranger when you come through the door but you won't leave one, that's for sure, Martha sees to that." Martha interrupted with a cup of coffee and a menu. The fellow on my left introduced himself almost like he was a church greeter. "I don't remember names," he said, "but I do know my own." He told me his name but I don't remember it. He welcomed me to the breakfast bunch and said that it seemed like the same crowd comes in every morning.

Martha was back, "Okay Bob, what'll it be? You look like a Waffle and ham guy to me." I was about to say something about some eggs and bacon but my coffee hadn't stimulated my faculties sufficiently to quicken my tongue. Martha shouted in typical Waffle House style, "Bob wants a waffle and ham, and honey, do you want it over light or golden brown?" Well, I didn't know I had a choice, I thought you just get a waffle and that's it, no medium or well done. I responded, "Golden brown, please, and could you make it 5 minutes before you put it on. I'm not awake yet." Martha looked right at me, "Well, assertive too, I like that about a man, knows what he wants and goes after it." I hadn't been in the place more than 3 minutes and already I was the discussion of a psychology seminar. There was a general consensus, "That's right Martha, that's right," from the group on my end of the counter.

The cook said, "Where are you from?" I told him that I was from

Raleigh and that I came to Richmond to study for a week at Union Seminary. When they learned that I was Presbyterian the fun began. Martha shoved a waffle and ham my way and topped off my coffee. I had the feeling that I just might have to eat breakfast there every morning. A woman in the booth by the window chimed in, "What's the difference between a Baptist and a Presbyterian?" I knew I was getting set up for some fun by the question so I gave a light answer, "Not much, the Presbyterians like to save water when we baptize somebody instead of using those 500 gallon baptism tanks the Baptists use. We like the preaching to end right on time so we can beat the Baptist to the restaurants, plus we think that when you get saved once, you're saved for good." I could hardly finish my sentence before the place hummed with responses, most of them humorous. Those that sounded serious I answered lightly and moved on with the good-natured crowd.

By the time I finished my waffle I felt a little bit like I had been to church even though I had left Saint Andrews miles back in my rear view mirror. I found warm faces and friendly conversation. I was welcomed from the moment I opened the door. There was Martha and her regulars. She could count on them and they could count on her. There were clear messages being passed along in the Waffle House that included acceptance and, I believe, love too. And the eggs, bacon, grits and waffles, well, they surely were as close to communion as I've ever known in a secular place. Maybe Martha worked the mystery of God in her holy place, the Waffle House.

Buddy and the Snake

Every morning at our Stonegate Drive home in Raleigh, Anne and I would get up, put on the coffee and let our dog, Buddy, out of the side door. He was a black cockerpoo who always knew his routine. Buddy was supposed to take care of his business and then retrieve for us the morning paper, which was down the driveway 180 feet from the house. We enjoyed watching him pick up the paper in his mouth and proudly make the trip back to us waiting at the top of the driveway. The way he carried the paper with his head held up high made him look, if for only a moment, like he might be the royal pooch of a king instead of the shaggy mutt that he really was. But we always praised him and gave him his bowl of food to show our thanks. We tried to teach Buddy some other tricks too. We worked hard trying to get him to bark on command and turn in a circle, but he just looked at us like we were short on intelligence and could do those tricks ourselves, but to forget about his going along with the whole idea. And most discouraging of all, Buddy wouldn't chase a ball and bring it back to us, the simplest, most natural trick a dog can do. But no, not Buddy. He would stand by our feet and watch the ball bounce down the driveway without even the slightest bit of interest.

But Buddy was faithful. Whenever we returned home after being away for a few hours he jumped and barked as if we had been gone for a week. Frankly, I don't think that Buddy knew the difference between one hour and 8 hours. And when he made his trip each morning to pick up the morning paper, he didn't know the difference between a Sunday and a Wednesday, but he was faithful. But there was this particular Sunday morning when I wished he had chosen a Wednesday to get into big time trouble.

On this particular Sunday morning I let Buddy out for his routine. When he picked up the paper in his mouth he made a couple of gallant strides back toward the house. That's when it happened. Buddy lost all of his royal appearance, dropped his paper, sniffed his nose up high, and made a mad dash towards something in the grass near the mailbox. In no more time than it takes a hound dog to chase a rabbit I saw Buddy on his stomach rubbing both sides of his face on something, we didn't know what. With great curiosity I quickly put my cup of coffee down on the kitchen table and ran down the driveway. I saw Buddy turn over on his back and continue massaging something that was obviously a great gift to his canine nature. Then I feared the worse. I had seen this behavior a time or two with my boyhood dog. It must be something dead! I screamed at Buddy hoping to get him to leave his stinking treasure and run away. But he was determined to get as much out of this filthy snake as he could. The snake was 7 or 8 feet long. I didn't stop long enough to measure it. The huge snake had been dead at least 24 hours or more.

As of that moment Buddy had become the brother to a snake. His smell was nauseating. How could he be so ignorant, so stupid to think that wallowing in some stinking dead creature was a smart way to have some fun? Why did his brain give way to irrational behavior? How could Buddy forget that we had just shampooed his curly coat on Saturday afternoon, leaving him shiny and proud? Didn't he have any pride? My questions seemed to fall on the dog's deaf ears.

So I grabbed him by the collar, forcefully dragged him off the snake and pulled him up the driveway to the house. I told Anne to get Buddy's leash and she hooked it around his neck. By now both of us began to smell like Buddy. It was awful. But Buddy seemed quite happy as if there was no problem at all. I figured that he felt dressed to the max and was proud of the dog show. I had the temptation to put Buddy in the garage and just leave him there but I decided that the longer he was totally objectionable the longer it would take to get him presentable again. So Anne got the shampoo and hosed Buddy down in the front yard. I knew that this job was going to be a really big one so Anne poured on the shampoo like we were millionaires with only one hour to live. Buddy's sin was going to require some major cleansing and forgiveness to get him right with the world. So after a thorough scrubbing from head to tail and toe, we hosed him down real well. We fully anticipated his shaking off the water in the joy of being the cleanest dog in town.

But no, not Buddy. He still reeked with "dead snake perfume," almost like we hadn't washed him at all. So we repeated the "cleansing of his soul" shampoo all over again, putting extra time on his face and legs. When we rinsed him the second time he smelled no better. But the worse thing of all was that now our hands also smelled terribly. We put Buddy in the garage and left him. We showered ourselves but it seemed to do no good. It was time for a quick breakfast and review of my sermon but I couldn't eat anything due to the smell on my hands. So Anne and I dressed, went to church and hid back in my office prior to the service. The elders came by to pray with us and when I explained the cause of the odor in the room, they all declined to hold hands in the circle as we normally did. I entered worship without shaking hands with anyone and when worship was over I quickly scampered back to my office again.

I've thought about that day as the years go by. Sometimes it's just a humorous story in my life and Anne's, just a bit of life that you laugh about when you're having a good time looking back over your shoulder with family or friends. And as much as I don't like storytellers and writers finding a moral in everything, this one is too rich to let go. Like Buddy, we also find ourselves attracted to behavior and thoughts that will cut our spiritual legs out from under us unless we are "wise as serpents and innocent as doves." Ever since the Garden of Eden we are neither wise nor innocent. Once we have sinned, we may be quickly forgiven and we might get a total cleansing, but it still takes a long time for the sinner to adjust to his/her new identity with God and his neighbors. In my own life I have occasionally found myself in disbelief over something I've done, or worse, something I've influenced someone else to do that was wrong. I'm glad that Jesus is my Savior. I've given Him a lot to do during my life. He's washed me cleaner than Buddy ever got.

The Waters of My Mental Illness

In The Shallow Waters Of My Mental Illness

I've enjoyed the luxury of being an optimist most of my life. Being a winner on many championship athletic teams and being elected as president of several school and church groups during my youth laid the groundwork for the blessing that would be mine for years to come. But simultaneously I found myself walking in the shallow waters of mental illness. I was not swept away by its current early on but in numerous periods of my life I fell face down into it. I believed my thinking and feelings were like every kid's but often I felt isolated and alone. Life for me was bittersweet, as it was with all kids I suppose, but looking back I can see that the murky waters that I waded in clouded my daily steps and my future to come.

Perhaps the serious asthma that plagued my childhood was the start-up cause of my attention deficit. The medicine given to me several times nightly for more than twelve years or more was ipecac, primarily a sedative, and it made me lethargic, not just during the night but also during the morning hours. In school I had to fight to stay awake. Our family doctor made frequent night visits to our home to check on my breathing and to ensure that I had sufficient ipecac to last me till morning. My father's chain smoking aggravated my asthma but in the 1940's and 50's no one understood the relationship between respiratory illness and cigarette smoking.

A very significant event occurred when I was 12 years old. During a visit with a friend in another city I was sexually abused by a 19 year-old woman. As a religious boy I immediately felt that I had been violated and that my virtue had been stolen from me. I felt ashamed. My abuser told me that it was my fault and to never say anything to anyone. The guilt that I felt went with me wherever

I went. I felt damaged. I believed that I needed constant forgiveness for being a part of this act that was forced on me. I thought I was going to lose my sanity along with my virginity. The trauma brought me stress that no child should have to go though. And it's no surprise that I hid the story from everyone, just like my abuser told me to do by saying, "this is our secret." I held on to the secret for 45 years before I told a counselor the story of my abuse. Only God knows how fully this trauma has effected my life, however it is certain that it created a sensitivity in me that helps me understand pain that others feel.

When I read Jeremiah 29:11, "For I know the plans I have for you," says the Lord, "plans for your welfare and not for evil, to give you a future and a hope," I was convinced of God's hand on my life. My dedication to God and my love of people led me to a commitment in a vocation in ministry when I was 16 years old. I'm convinced that even at that young age God transformed my hurt, anger and isolation into an expression of service and love.

At times I looked healthy on the outside when I was troubled on the inside. I retained an unconscious desire to please everyone around me. I worked harder than was required. I burned the candle at both ends. The long hours and hard work were self- imposed. Through Jr. and Sr. High Schools I had a paper route that meant getting up at 4:30 every morning. After school I played sports and was on five state championship teams in track and baseball. My Pony League baseball team went to the World Series in Pennsylvania. I was encouraged by friends to run for president of the High School student body and I was elected. To earn a free lunch, I made sandwiches at a deli during lunch break during my senior year.

I worked at the Highway Department every afternoon of my senior year. After supper I studied my homework until 11:00 or until I fell asleep at my desk. On weekends I dated most Friday and Saturday nights and I never missed church activities in the morning and at night. When I crammed my life's activities into 19 hours a day I felt boosted by a false pride over being able to be so influential with so many people. I accepted the praise that I received without thinking about how it might be affecting me in a negative way. I was walking in the shallow waters of my mental illness early in my life.

As I began my first semester in Presbyterian College in 1960 I continued to have an overwhelming strength for life. One new feature of my life, however, was being depressed like clockwork during May and December. Without any knowledge about mental illness I assumed I was fatigued but resting didn't seem to lift my spirit. Even a few weeks away from school didn't make a difference. Slowly I would return to my hectic schedule. I was on both a work scholarship and an athletic scholarship in track and baseball. I pressed my classes into a busy schedule including 18 hours weekly working in the dining hall. As soon as class was over at noon on Saturdays I thumbed a ride to Charlotte to be with my new girlfriend, Brownie Allen. It was always a great time but catching rides back to Presbyterian was frequently dangerous and difficult. Often I would arrive back at my dorm at 11:00 P.M. Sunday needing to spend at least 3 hours on homework. The shallow waters of mental illness stirred under my feet. I was unable to see where I stood. When my athletic scholarship was denied because of the Board's cutback in spring sports I lost the money I needed for tuition. With anger I left P.C. and began life at USC. It was a painful loss.

Life in Columbia at USC was demanding, especially since I worked 40 hours a week at Allied Chemical to pay for my college expenses. It meant that my grades suffered. My relationship with God suffered too. I was taking a full load of classes. I attended worship every Sunday night. I felt great pressure to manage my life in the way I did. The pressure did not come from anyone else. It was internal. I received high accolades from so many people. Their praise put me on a pedestal. I believed that everyone was telling me how great I was. I felt like I was able to accomplish everything I tried to do. The signs of bipolar disorder are easy to see now but when I was 20, all I could see was another mountain to climb.

During my college years my mother spent long months in deep depressions. She was given ECT's (electro convulsive therapy) that were attempts to lift her back into a pleasant state of mind. But the mental chains that held her down were slow to release her. The medicine chosen by her psychiatrist was Valium. Fifty years later we know it was inadequate to treat uni-polar depression. It was certainly not enough help for someone who might have had a bipolar disorder, which I think would have been my mother's diagnosis if the psychiatrist had spent more time listening to her and less time writing prescriptions for her. Since I was living at home during 3 of my years at USC in Columbia in the early 60's I added the heavy responsibility of caring for mother. Though I did so with love, caring for her narrowed my window of sleep to about four hours a night. Normalcy for me was keeping my pace at any cost. It almost cost me my life.

In my herculean effort to juggle so many important parts of my life I lost balance of the healthy expectations a person might have for himself. Carolina classes, 40 hours at Allied Chemical, homework, religious devotion, caring for mother, they all combined to make my life barely manageable. In my sophomore year I ended my two-year relationship with Brownie Allen. I rekindled an old love with Anne Reynolds who became the light in my darkness for years to come.

Even with Anne's wisdom and God's help I could not see that I was wading in the shallow waters of mental illness.

Something had to give and it did. In May of 1964 I went to the dean's office at USC to pick up my hat and my gown for graduation. He told me I was 20 hours short and would not be able to graduate. I was sure that he had made a mistake. He countered my objection and showed me proof. How had I lost track of such important information? I remember leaving his office in a silent rage. God only knows how I avoided a total crash that summer.

I took 8 hours of classes during the summer, worked at Allied Chemical full time and wondered if I would be allowed to enter Columbia Theological Seminary in Atlanta in the fall. I still needed 12 hours to graduate but the Dean at CTS made an exception and allowed me to enter school if I agreed to finish the remaining 12 hours for graduation at USC by the end of the year. With my high energy I made the commitment. So for the first semester at CTS I took 16 hours plus 8 hours of USC correspondence courses.

It astounds me when I look back on those days. Graduate school alone was demanding but adding undergraduate courses on top was a foolish decision. But my life was on a roll, and besides, I didn't want my self-image of being King On The Mountain to roll down the hill where normal people live. I almost succumbed to the pressure but I never let anyone know it. I was up 19 hours a day. I made B's on everything the first semester that proved to me that I was the leader of the pack. I felt almost invincible. I was a bright fellow but not that bright. I was walking in the shallow waters of mental illness, very close to a dangerous drop-off.

Seminary was much more demanding than my college career. Since I finished only one of my USC courses I would have to work again on a 24 credit load the second semester of Seminary. Perhaps I should have been able to understand that my emotional lows and highs were interrupting each other on the way up and down but I couldn't see it happening.

In August of 1965 Anne and I were married. It was the best decision of my life. There was a new joy and challenge for living every day. Life was good. But I had to face that even with Anne on my team that I was still struggling to maintain a healthy lifestyle. When she went to bed at 9 P.M. in order to be rested for teaching her fourth grade class, I usually went to the library until closing time at 11 P.M. From there I went to the "Dunkin Dine" restaurant where I studied until 1 P.M. I became a smoker in my second year of seminary and smoked a half pack of cigarettes every night while I studied.

Truthfully, I was hiding from the crowd. I survived the three semesters after we were married but the last semester of seminary I bottomed out. After months of mania I became depressed. I was paranoid and remember standing in our third floor apartment and fearfully watching students changing classes, hoping no one would see me hiding behind the curtains. I would not have been able to graduate on time if it hadn't been for Bill Barron. Bill knocked at my door one morning and during his visit reminded me of how everyone was missing me. He encouraged me to come back to classes.

Since the semester was nearing an end I again had to appeal to the Dean to let me take exams. Somehow I made acceptable grades on all of them. I can't explain the miracle in my good grades that semester, unless God decided to intervene. Though I graduated on time I knew that I had run into something serious and threatening to my health. I didn't know I was bipolar. My mental illness was unnamed but it would affect my entire life to come. I was walking in the shallow waters of mental illness. Mental illness is experienced from within where our soul struggles to understand its conflicting desires to be both healthy in our quests and yet to be unhealthy in our behavior. It can come like a strong breeze or like a tornado, spinning its damage without rhyme or reason.

When I accepted the call to the Lakewood Presbyterian Church in Jacksonville, Florida, in August of 1967 and I realized that I had been given perhaps the best call of my seminary class. I felt thrilled. We moved from Atlanta to Jacksonville, bought a home near the church, and I felt better than I could remember feeling in years. We were ready for life. I went to a routine Presbytery Exam Meeting in order to be allowed to be ordained. I was told if I didn't know the answer totally to say "I don't know" so that we could move on to the next question. The actual committee was on vacation so a haphazard, substitute committee, without knowledge of their task, did the verbal questioning. I knew many answers but I admitted I didn't know the full answer to some questions like, "Compare Isaiah 50:4 with Philippians 2:14," along with many similar questions that seemed to require a photographic memory. So on many such questions I said "I don't know." I found out how absurd the test was when I was told I failed the test.

My embarrassment and anger was almost unmanageable. I had to postpone my ordination for three months until I passed the exam. I felt that failing my exam would express to the congregation that I was ill prepared for my task as their Associate Minister. Passing the exam given by the "official," appointed committee was quite easy, but the misfortune of those months ripped at the seams of my self-esteem. I was very depressed for several months but I think I hid much of my feelings from the church members. Lurking in the back of my mind was the truth that all of the classes I missed and all the time I spent in unproductive study at CTS had come back to haunt me. Though I adjusted to my work at Lakewood, our five years there included bi-annual depressions and periods of accomplishment that were extra-ordinary.

In the spring of 1972 I began to feel called out of the Lakewood church. I didn't know how it would unfold. Mark was almost 4 years old and Julie was 2. I was restless and hypo-manic. My unnamed bipolar illness, though of moderate strength, was revving up for another fast race around the track. I felt invincible. I believed I could accomplish anything. My illness picked up steam and took my personal ethics to the brink of disaster. Anne and I began walking down a long road of sadness. I was depressed. Counseling was slow in helping us. I felt lost and considered a separation.

When the call came from the Hope Presbyterian Church in Clearwater in August of 1972, we both thought that the change might buy us some time to revive our relationship. The move slowly brought new life to us. Our relationship prospered little by little. It required a year's intensive counseling but eventually I felt good to be home again. Because of the adversity we were stronger and ready for the next phase of our lives. The waters of my bipolar illness receded, if only temporarily.

However, my bipolar illness continued to play roulette with every part of my life for the next 10 years. For long periods of time, sometimes for several months consecutively, I was high as a kite. I had super energy and accomplished the work of two people. I was highly successful in my church's ministry, in Presbytery's life, in international missions in Haiti, and especially in my music ministry with Tom, singing contemporary Christian songs around the South. But much of the energy for my success came from my unidentified bipolar illness. I again found myself burning the candle at both ends, working until 2:00 A.M. writing songs and sermons. Spending time with Anne, Mark and Julie was important to me and with my manic behavior I had plenty of energy to enjoy them during the daytime hours.

I felt very high in my mood most of the time from 1972 to 1980 with clockwork bouts of depression in May and December. But in 1980 I felt depressed for a three-month period and wrongly defined it as a marital issue. After extended counseling and a renewed understanding of life I adjusted to a workable role as husband and father. Anne was never the real problem. It was my bipolar illness, still unidentified at the time, that was driving me toward unhealthy goals. If I had understood what was going on in my brain we might have avoided our long periods of marital conflict. Looking back I'm certain that my extreme highs and lows were the shallow waters of a mental illness that would eventually flood my life 28 years later.

My musician buddy, Tom Schneider, and I strongly discussed going full time with our Contemporary Christian sound. It looked so promising and alluring to us. It would have travel, excitement, praise and friendship wrapped into one vocational package for the 80's. I was 40 years old and ready for the next step in ministry. I didn't see the temptation but Anne pointed out the danger for my health and our marriage. Her wisdom was hard to accept but she was right.

However, my feet were still itching when the Medical Benevolence Foundation offered me a position with its international mission work for the Presbyterian Church. It was a sincere call to do ministry on a different scale. Anne agreed. The next 3 and 1/2 years took me around the world to mission stations in rural villages and in large cities. It was exciting but I experienced depressions that bounced off my highs as the months went by. In 1987 I felt a burdening fatigue and opened myself to the possibility of serving another church.

In The Deep Waters of My Mental Illness

When we were called to the Saint Andrews Presbyterian Church in 1987 Anne and I could clearly see that God was giving us the church of a lifetime. From the beginning of our ministry in Raleigh, N.C. the congregation was living out its faith in extraordinary ways. We developed excellent programs in education, youth ministry, music, worship, missions and adult support groups. The most astounding fact was a program that my associate, Craig Holladay, developed that assimilated 1800 new members during my 12 years there. In our Saturday night and Sunday morning services we enjoyed worshipping with approximately 1600 members.

I enjoyed better health for the first five years in Raleigh, experiencing more moderate mood swings that were manageable. But two back surgeries in 1992 kept me out of ministry for six months and a serious neck surgery in 1995 interrupted my ministry for 3 more months. My staff picked up my responsibilities but I experienced depression again. The pain from the 3 surgeries required that I use pain pills and steroids for many weeks. My doctors told me that taking my medications over a long period of time, combined with steroids and the high stress from a rapidly growing church, likely caused the highs and lows of my bipolar illness to widen. There were mornings when I felt my mood sink rapidly, yet soar like a kite in the afternoon. During my highs I had a tremendous sense of sincere spirituality. I felt holy, set apart, qualified for ministry to a great degree. It is true that through the Holy Spirit we are mentored and inspired but I felt that my inspiration for Saint Andrews was greater than the inspiration others had been given. I was manic then, though I was blind to the truth.

During the 1995 through 1998 period the church staff of 22 and the

250

church officers were planning to relocate to a larger space nearby because of overcrowding in worship, education and parking. One incident shook me. In a meeting with church leaders a man accused me of wanting to build a mega-church instead of serving the people in our current membership on our original property. Without thinking I screamed at him at the top of my lungs, declaring his assessment of me wrong. I knew then that something had come loose in my system. My rage drowned my self-concept.

I lost faith with myself from time to time. Although my powerful anger never exploded in public again, at home I began to rage quietly into a pillow, muffling the screams of my mind. I sent my feelings to a dark closet with the hope that I could hold myself together without anyone seeing the crack in my armor. That behavior of keeping my crisis to myself was exactly the opposite of my lifelong teaching about our need to be vulnerable in relationships with one another. But I believed that with prayer and rest God would drain off my psychic pain. But the knee deep waters of my illness were threatening to rise above my shoulders.

In early 1998 I bought paints, red, blue, green, yellow and mixed them brightly. I think I was trying to drown my self-perceived ugliness in lovely color. Some of the loveliest paintings I've ever done were in the year 1998.

In the fall of 1998 we put the question of relocation to the congregation and the vote was 57% to 43% to relocate. We determined that the 14% margin of the majority was not strong enough to go forward with a church wide fund raising campaign. We had set 80% as our minimum in order to move forward. The loss was a major setback for the church officers and me. On the day of the vote I asked a pro and a con speaker to outline their positions regarding relocation. I didn't speak for or against on that day, believing the victory was easily in hand. I believe my judgment was shortsighted and that my voice would have handily won the day. I took responsibility for the loss. We had worked for three years on the project and had bought 17 acres for moving forward. We still had a great congregation of 1500 with 4 services where 1600 people worshipped with us every weekend. But we just couldn't handle any more growth. There was nowhere to park. My stress was very high.

In my lifelong Christian experience I felt at one with God. Yet in late 1998 I discovered a shift, not only emotionally, but also spiritually. Ever since I was a boy I had a keen sense of God within me. I knew that God was accessible to me. God lived in my soul. Jesus was a friend who loved me more than I loved him. I felt so alive when I was in church or in my prayer time. I knew that the Holy Spirit was living within me.

But my soul slowly began to drown in the rising river. It took me longer to write a sermon or to prepare for a class. Often I stayed home and napped for two hours, dreading the thought of having to return to the office. In reality I was unable to accomplish the reading necessary to help me prepare well for classes or sermons. My heart was into the church's development but my mind was shutting down. In general I had more difficulty in thinking rationally. From day to day I found myself undecided about critical decisions. When I preached I felt like I was speaking through a curtain, wondering if anyone was listening. Almost unbelievably I have been told that my preaching during those days was even more effective than when I was healthy. Perhaps it's because I had to depend on God more than at any previous time. I was not, however, able to comprehend the miraculous quality of my preaching. It no longer satisfied my soul.

I wondered if God had cast me off the Christian ship like Jonah had been when he was running away from God's order to go to Nineveh. My emotions became unpredictable. I got sicker by the week. I hated waking up each morning. The shallow waters of my mental illness were moving deeper under my chin. My paranoia grew and I thought that people knew how depressed I was. I couldn't wait to take my medicine each night and try to relax. I began to stay up later and later each night and my energy level dropped dramatically. I went from high to low at least weekly but my lows rudely bulldozed my highs against my will.

My entire feel for my responsibilities crashed. I didn't have the self-control or the self-determination to manage the church or my own needs. My confusion grew by the week. Anne, my wife, who had been standing strong beside me through it all, understood that a drastic change needed to occur. She and our adult children, Mark and Julie, gathered around me with the love and understanding that got my attention. The elders generously gave me the 3 months leave of absence that I requested in January 1999. The complexity and sadness of leaving Raleigh and moving to Columbia, S.C. broke what little spirit I had left. My life as I had known it was over. My meds had failed. The dam filled with all of my thinking, feeling and energy broke free. Anne, Mark and Julie were there to channel me toward better health. At least I was "decision free."

My brother Bill and his wife, Joanna, welcomed us with open arms into their home in Columbia. I don't know what we would have done without their love. I began a long series of ECT treatments (electro convulsive therapy.) that some psychiatrists agree can help lift people out of deep depressions. My memory was affected during that time, partly due to the ECT's and likely due to the depression itself. My memory loss is still is a problem for me today. What I do remember is the struggle to get my brain out of neutral. I couldn't move it enough to bring in necessary information for normal decisions. Clothes, faces and places seemed gray. There was one humorous release about living those months at Bill and Jo's. It was ice cream. After supper each evening we ate huge bowls full of ice cream. My weight jumped up 25 pounds.

In April, when my depression only deepened, my family insisted that I resign from Saint Andrews and spend full time getting well. Not just Anne, Mark, and Julie but also my extended family urged me to resign. I held out hope but eventually knew that my family's wisdom was best. They agreed that I was no longer prepared for ministry. In July of 1999 I resigned. It was the hardest decision I ever made.

We bought a house and moved to Columbia. I was given more ECT's but my health didn't improve. The frequent flip-flop of my depression and mania was severely un-nerving. In my serious consideration of suicide I visited two pawn stores on Assembly Street late one afternoon and handled four different pistols. When I tried to purchase one I was told that the store was closing and also that there was a two-day waiting period before I could have the gun. That state law saved my life.

Our friends in Washington, Mac and Bobbie Macdonald, introduced me to Dr. Fred Goodwin, the Director of the National Institute of Mental Health, who diagnosed me correctly as having a bipolar disorder. I exploded when I learned that my diagnosis had been wrong and that my prescriptions for over a year had not been helpful. My mania convinced me, however, that my excessive energy was from an ambivalent God when it was only the opposite side of depression. The frequent flip-flop from depression to mania was severely un-nerving. I considered suicide once again.

254

About three years after we had moved to Columbia I began working as a volunteer in Burnside Elementary School, first of all with Nancy Archie in first grade, then with Anne's sister, Gayle Troutman in kindergarten. Both assignments were beneficial in getting me out of our house, offering me healthy interaction with the public. But it seemed that nothing could take away the rollercoaster that soared and fell without my permission.

I believed that God was not going to rescue me. I had worked hard to get well and I had made very little progress. Since I had been a faithful servant all my life I thought God had betrayed me. I lost touch with my inner self and felt hopeless. "By the waters of Babylon, I sat down and wept." Not actually, since my tears had dried up. Thankfully, one night I had a dream that changed my entire viewpoint of life. I was in a canoe drifting downstream toward a high waterfall, fighting the current for hours, trying to keep from going over the falls. When I reached the point of exhaustion I decided to stop fighting and instead drift over the falls, accepting whatever might become of me.

Jesus was on the bank when I came up out of the water. I was willing to die if it meant release from my fatigue and pain. For the next several years I took the dream to mean that I was fighting too hard by my own power to get well and I needed to relax, follow my doctor's orders, and patiently wait for Jesus to walk on the water to me. My medicines began to adjust. The dream taught me that I was no longer the person I use to be. The old man is gone and the new one has come. It was a dream of a lifetime.

So I faced my aloneness. I no longer cursed God for my mental imprisonment. I took my Bible from the shelf. I let life come to me without always thinking that I should have been dealt a better hand of cards. My anger transformed into a knowledge that the waterfall dream was from God and that I was living on the right side of hope. When the dream didn't quickly eradicate my anger I stopped kicking myself. When my journaling froze I laid it aside until I thawed out a bit. I stopped feeling guilty when I refused an invitation to be with other people. I didn't attend worship often but that became okay for me. My prayers seem to hit a ceiling but the ceiling was only in my head. I was in the water, waiting on Jesus to save me. It seemed like a long wait, and it was. I still wonder why it took so many years to be given good health again.

Five years ago I became a good swimmer, you might say. Many key people began to invite me out and I began to accept their invitations. Tom Beason, my Florida buddy, has phoned weekly for more years than I can remember. He's one of my soul brothers. Charley Bryan is another soul friend. He asked me out for lunch one day and we've enjoyed lunch every week for 6 years. My brothers, John and Bill, and their wives, Janet and Joanna, have stayed close by me since the beginning of my illness. John has listened long and well to me all through my illness. Bill has given us wise financial counsel. He and Joanna have shared their beach home with us many times. Our son, Mark, and his wife, Ruth, have constantly stayed in touch with loving encouragement. Our daughter, Julie, and her husband, Adrian, are committed with their love and support. The birth of their son, Nathan Henry and their daughter, Lydia Evelyn, truly boosted my spirits.

Jim Reynolds, Anne's brother, has dropped by to check on us every week. He and his wife, Judy, have made their beach home available for our relaxation. Anne's sister, Gayle, invited me to be a volunteer in her kindergarten class where I spent 5 enjoyable years. Her husband, Ron, has been available for counsel on many important purchases. Ross Roggensack phoned me from Raleigh every week of my illness, usually just to give me a chance to talk. Mabel Duke Weeks phoned every week prior to her death in 2011. Loretta Bishop, whose life inspired this book, along with her husband Lamar, kept in touch over the last two years. Linda Olson, my therapist, understood me when I was confused about all of life. She helped me rethink who I am and how that knowledge could help me make workable choices for the future. My psychiatrist, Dr. Carl Kinard, has been masterful in his care for me, changing my medicines as often as my behavior changed.

Over the last two years, 2010 to 2012, I've begun to feel the turnaround that my dream offered. My physical health is better. I enjoy friends and family and look forward to being with them. I play my harmonicas every day. At times I do feel paranoid about getting in large groups so worship is still troubling for me. Spiritually I feel more at home with God and myself. Reading my Bible is not a daily habit for me, but I'm getting there. I'm a speaker for the National Alliance on Mental Illness that gives me the opportunity to do something to help the community become aware of the needs of the mentally ill. I'm thankful to God for the ability to speak in public again, even though it's stressful for me.

I've spent the last twelve years on a pilgrimage to find the person I'm becoming. The journey has been risky and painful. It's also been rejuvenating and mysterious. The mystery is God's. The re-making of myself remains a puzzle I don't think I'll ever completely solve. I've stopped asking why I have to go through my mental illness. Since I'm always recovering from my illness, never fully recovered, I want to know what will best maintain my health. I also want to stay in touch with ways that I can encourage others who are struggling with an illness like mine.

Anne, my always faithful and encouraging wife, knows more about adversity than perhaps I do. Anne is a woman with remarkable love and strength who understands that our growth in life is ultimately due to the way God meets us in our adversity. Anne's unwillingness to concede her part in my life is not only why we're still married but also why I'm still alive. Only a few can weather giant storms and still be sailing when the sun reappears. Anne is God's proof that it can be done.

What's around the corner? I don't know. I do know that I'm feeling better now than at anytime in the past 12 years. I've got good friends and a loving family. When life's waters rose above my knees and up to my nose I found strength all about me. It's a wonderful gift to see the Lord's work in me still. I hope this book will be a life preserver to many people who are unsure that a brighter day is in their future.

I pray that each of us who are seeking greater spiritual health will find a way to get in touch with our own stories. Some are up building, some are not, but all of them offer us the wholeness God wants us to discover.